PRAISE FOR

OLD TESTAMENT SURVEY II

"Nathan LeMaster puts in the hands of pastors and laity alike an accessible survey of the Old Testament. For each biblical book, he highlights the purpose, themes, and literary structure, while noting key background information. This is a welcome resource for those wanting to read Holy Scripture with more care and detail."

— Ethan C. Jones
Don and Helen Bryant Chair of Old Testament
Associate Professor of Old Testament and Hebrew
New Orleans Baptist Theological Seminary

"Every Christian's spiritual journey should include many trips through the Old Testament. For both the first-time visitor and the seasoned traveler, Dr. Nathan LeMaster's volume on the Old Testament is an excellent travel guide!"

— Keith Essex
Emeritus Professor of Bible Exposition, The Master's Seminary

Titles in the Christian Life Series

Published in 2023

Heaven and Hell: A Survey of the Biblical Doctrines of Personal Eschatology (Kevin Zuber)

The Forgotten Attributes of God: God's Nature and Why It Matters (Peter Sammons)

Old Testament Survey I: Genesis to Esther (Nathan LeMaster)

Well Done: A Strategy for Life Stewardship (Reagan Rose)

Becoming a Worthy Reader: How to Read and Study the Bible (Kevin Zuber)

Published in 2024

New Testament Survey I: Matthew to Acts & Johannine Literature (Nathan LeMaster)

Gender and Sexuality (Michael Riccardi)

Published in 2025

The Church and Church Membership (John MacArthur)

Old Testament Survey II (Nathan LeMaster)

Coming in 2026 and beyond (tentative titles)

Salvation and Sanctification (author TBD)

The Spiritual Disciplines (author TBD)

Spiritual Leadership (author TBD)

The Creeds of the Church (author TBD)

New Testament Survey II (Nathan LeMaster)

Spiritual Gifts and Service (author TBD)

The Person of God or *The Authority of Scripture* (author TBD)

Biblical Reconciliation (author TBD)

Marriage and Family Counseling (author TBD)

Discipling and Mentoring (author TBD)

Global and Local Missions (author TBD)

BIBLE KNOWLEDGE

Old Testament Survey II

Job to Malachi

NATHAN LEMASTER

CLC PUBLICATIONS
Fort Washington, PA 19034

Old Testament Survey II: Job to Malachi
The Christian Life Series

Published by CLC Publications

USA: P.O. Box 1449, Fort Washington, PA 19034
www.clcpublications.com

UK: Kingsway CLC Trust
Unit 5, Glendale Avenue, Sandycroft, Flintshire, CH5 2QP
www.equippingthechurch.com

ISBN (paperback): 978-1-61958-410-5
ISBN (ebook): 978-1-61958-415-0

Printed in the United States of America

Italics in Scripture quotations, if not original to the NASB, are the emphasis of the author.

Contents

Foreword 7

Introduction: Poetry, Wisdom Literature, and Prophecy 9

1. Job 13
2. Psalms 25
3. Proverbs 33
4. Ecclesiastes 41
5. Song of Solomon 49
6. Isaiah 53
7. Jeremiah 59
8. Lamentations 67
9. Ezekiel 71
10. Daniel 77
11. Hosea 85
12. Joel 91
13. Amos 95

14. Obadiah 99

15. Jonah 103

16. Micah 109

17. Nahum 113

18. Habakkuk...117

19. Zephaniah 123

20. Haggai 127

21. Zechariah..131

22. Malachi 135

Foreword

Dr. Nathan LeMaster (PhD, Cambridge) serves as Assistant Professor of Old Testament at The Master's Seminary. He brings us the second volume dedicated to Bible Survey of the Old Testament. Many, even within the church, underestimate the importance of the Old Testament. Too often, believers neglect the rich history found in the Old Testament because they deem it to be impractical or irrelevant.

B.B. Warfield once said, "The Old Testament may be likened to a chamber richly furnished but dimly lighted; the introduction of light brings into it nothing which was not in it before; but it brings out into clearer view much of what is in it but was only dimly or even not at all perceived before.

"The mystery of the Trinity is not revealed in the Old Testament; but the mystery of the Trinity underlies the Old Testament revelation, and here and there almost comes into view. Thus the Old Testament revelation of God is not corrected by the fuller revelation that follows it, but only perfected, extended, and enlarged."

The richness of the Old Testament is best understood and appreciated by New Testament believers, for the Old Testament reveals Christ. The Old Testament doesn't just "point forward" to Christ; it reveals Him. This book covers major themes and events of the books of Job through Malachi, tracing the major developments and rich history, chapter-by-chapter, highlighting unique and important features to help believers as they study each book.

Whether you have time-tested experience in ministry, or you're a new believer, we expect this book will provide both rigor and refreshment to help you in your labor for the Lord.

Peter Sammons, PhD, Series Editor
Author of *Reprobation and God's Sovereignty*
and *The Forgotten Attributes of God*

Introduction

Poetry, Wisdom Literature, and Prophecy

THE OLD TESTAMENT IS full of beautiful and intricate books that have often been neglected. Christians can easily relate to many of the psalms, and the proverbs are pearls of wisdom that are easy to apply to daily life. But in a book like Haggai or Joel we may not find clear application unless we put in diligent effort and work to understand the author's intention.

Different people have tried to divide the Old Testament in multiple ways throughout history. Perhaps the best way to divide the books is to see them in three categories.

The first category, and the most foundational, is the Pentateuch. These first five books of the Old Testament are the foundation on which everything else is laid. In many ways the rest of the Old Testament reiterates what is already taught in Genesis, Exodus, Leviticus, Numbers, and Deuteronomy.

The Pentateuch establishes God as the creator. It describes God's nature and how God interacts with His creation. It speaks to the problem of sin and the necessity of a Redeemer. It gives prophecy of a coming Redeemer who will bring with Him justice and righteousness. It speaks of the nature of God's holiness and how humans are to approach a holy God. The Pentateuch sets the foundation for all that is to come.

The second category is the Prophets. Historically, this category has the Former Prophets (Joshua, Judges, Samuel, and Kings) and the Latter Prophets. The Latter Prophets are also broken down into the Major Prophets (Isaiah, Jeremiah, Ezekiel) and the Minor Prophets (Hosea, Joel, Amos, Obadiah, Jonah, Micah, Nahum, Habakkuk, Zephaniah, Haggai, Zechariah, and Malachi).

Speaking broadly, the key characteristic of the Prophets is that they are a mouthpiece for God, speaking to the nation of Israel and calling that nation to repentance. The Prophets add insight and clarity, but their messages are based on what the Pentateuch has already said and commanded. Often, they do not give additional commands but just point the people back to the Pentateuch, calling the people to be faithful to their covenant with God.

The Prophets do add some additional insight concerning things such as the day of the Lord. But overall, they just call people to do what the Pentateuch has commanded them to do.

The third category is called the Writings. The Writings includes books that Christians today are more inclined to read devotionally. Many of these books are viewed as being more immediately applicable. This would include Psalms, Proverbs, and even beautiful little stories like Ruth. However, this category also includes difficult books, such as Lamentations, Job, and even the book of Daniel.

This category is often more approachable for Christians because the Writings tend to speak more to the individual. The Prophets speak directly to the nation of Israel, with implications for Gentile nations. But if the Prophets answer the question of how Israel is supposed to apply the Pentateuch, the Writings emphasize how the individual follower of God is to be faithful to the commands that God has laid out.

So many of the Psalms are cries of distress from one who is trying to follow God but who is encountering opposition and hostility. Job gives an in-depth look at the great suffering of a person who is described as being a blameless and upright man, one who fears God and turns away from evil. The writings incorporate a great deal of poetry—both poetry that exalts and praises God and poetry that cries out and laments the suffering of humanity.

A subcategory within the writings is Wisdom Literature. Some scholars debate what should be included in Old Testament Wisdom Literature. The best approach is to see three books making up this category: Job, Proverbs, and Ecclesiastes. These books focus on individual perspectives and ask life-altering questions. They have a common purpose: the quest for wisdom.

As we will explore in the chapters on these books, wisdom is not just shrewdness or skillful living, but it is the quest to understand how God has organized the world. How can suffering exist in a world that a good God has created? If people are destined to die, then why does anything in this life matter? How can it be that righteous people die early but wicked people seem to flourish? These are not easily answered questions, and they are only a sampling of questions that are seen in these Wisdom Literature books.

This book is the second volume in a survey of the Old Testament. To help simplify, we will keep the organization of the Old Testament that is reflected in our English Bibles.

Some people debate the organization and ordering of the books of the Old Testament. The organization of the books as we have them in our English Bibles is reflected in the Septuagint, which is the Greek translation of the Old Testament. The first volume of this survey of the Old Testament started in Genesis and ended with the book of Ruth. This second volume, though recognizing the three categories of Old Testament books listed above, will begin with the book of Job and end with Malachi.

As with the first volume, this book is intended to provide a helpful companion to the text of the Old Testament, which uncovers the authorial intention. The goal of Bible study should not primarily be to discover how the text affects us. The primary goal should be to understand what the authors tried to communicate to the reader. This is the authorial intention.

Only when we have uncovered the authorial intention do we then ask how the meaning affects our individual lives. Therefore, the purpose, structure, and themes of each book are important as they speak to why the authors of the Old Testament wrote the books.

The Old Testament holds a great variety of books; some seem more approachable than others. But every one is important to communicate God's character and how humans are to have relationship with God. No book, no text, is superfluous or unnecessary to the entirety of God's revelation. Therefore, we should approach each verse and every chapter with careful thought, prayerful consideration, and humility.

Before delving into our study, let us take the words of Isaiah 66:2 to heart: "But to this one I will look, to him who is humble and contrite of spirit, and who trembles at My word."

Reflection questions:

1. What books of the Old Testament do you gravitate toward, and what books do you find difficult to understand?

2. If we understand that every word and every verse of the Old Testament is important, how does that change how we study the Old Testament?

3. In what way is the Pentateuch a foundation for everything else that comes in the Old Testament? Should it be seen as the foundation for the New Testament as well? In what way?

1

Job

JOB IS INCLUDED WITH the Wisdom Literature books in the Old Testament. This also includes Ecclesiastes and Proverbs. These books are all bound together by the quest for wisdom, which has its foundation in the fear of God. Because Job deals with suffering in such a poignant way, this chapter will depart from the usual pattern. After the structure of the book is discussed, the themes will be examined. This will be followed by a lengthier discussion on the purpose which will take the place of a succinct purpose statement.

Job is a unique book and an interesting book, which requires time and dedicated attention to best understand. It is far removed from the twenty-first century, but the book has a timeless message that every individual must grapple with. The problem is suffering. Why is there suffering in the world? How can suffering exist in a world that has been created by a good God?

Many people who grew up in the church claim that this issue has driven them away from the church and from their faith. No question is more central to the human experience or cuts deeper into the human soul.

Death, devastation, destruction, and unimaginable pain are everyday elements of our world. Job grapples with this problem. The answers given in the book of Job are not fluffy, pat answers. They are answers from God's own mouth.

The story of Job is set in an early period in human history. Like the early portions of Genesis, Job seems to stand far from the world we see today. For example, Job 42 says that after Job's suffering he lived 140 more years. This is parallel with the patriarchal period, when lifespans were much longer than we see today.

Genesis says that Abraham lived to be 175 years old. Isaac lived to be 180 years old. Jacob lived to be 147 years old. After the fall in the garden of Eden, the lifespan of people began to degrade. So for Job to live 140 years after his suffering places the events within the early patriarchal period.

Not only did Job's lifespan point to a general time frame for the events of the book, but other things in the book point to this as well. For example, Job's wealth was not measured in terms of silver and gold but in terms of agriculture.

Chapter 1 says that before his suffering, he had 7,000 sheep, 3,000 camels, 500 yoke of oxen, and 500 female donkeys. Each of these animals spoke to a different aspect of Job's wealth. Job's wealth was multifaceted and extensive for his time. The text does not say Job was the wealthiest man, but the extent of his possessions points to his wealth and to his social status.

If we compare Job's wealth with Solomon's wealth, we see them described in different ways. Wealth was measured in different ways at different time periods. Solomon's wealth was measured in his beautiful palace, his gold and silver, and his extensive building projects. Job's wealth was measured in terms of agriculture.

The book of Job also stands out in the Old Testament because it does not have the Jewish elements that the other books do. The Pentateuch was not mentioned. Some overlapping terms were used, such as the Canaanites being viewed as tradesmen. Job 40:23 also refers to the Jordan river.

Despite a few overlapping terms, overall, the book of Job lacks Jewishness. This lack of focus on Israel did not diminish Job's relationship with God. Throughout the book, Job and his friends used God's covenant name, Yahweh. The debate between Job and his friends did not appeal to any previous scripture, including any of the books of Moses. Instead, the arguments appealed to natural theology, which we will examine in short order. Even though the Mosaic Law was not mentioned, Job made sacrifices on behalf of his children for their sins.

We do not see any mention of the author of the book of Job. The book does not tell us who this was. Many hypotheses have been put forth including Job himself being the author, Elihu being the author, or someone completely unnamed. We also do not see mention of a date for the writing of Job. The book does not claim that it was written in Job's lifetime. Since the book reveals the exact number of years Job lived after his suffering, we can understand that the book was finished after Job's death, but how long after is unknown.

The author of Job, under the inspiration of the Holy Spirit, gave explanation that Job knew nothing about. The author spoke of a day in heaven when the angels presented themselves before God, and Satan, called "The Accuser," came with them. The dialogue between God and Satan on two occasions resulted in Job's suffering.

However, Job never attributed his suffering to Satan. Job said that God gave and God took away. Job recognized God's sovereignty in everything that happened to him. But this is what brought the problem. If God was sovereign and all-powerful and all-knowing, then why was Job suffering?

An additional key element to note in the opening narrative is the description of Job. The author described him in verse 1 as being a blameless man, upright, one who feared God, and turned from evil. God himself described Job in the same words in Job 1:8. At the end of chapter 1, we see that Job did not sin in his response to his wealth being stripped away from him nor in his children being killed.

Job 2:10 also described Job: "In all this Job did not sin with his lips." This was right after Job was struck with a sickness described as boils reaching from the crown of Job's head to the soles of his feet. Job did not pretend that everything was okay. He was not removed from his suffering like someone who was only trying to think happy thoughts.

Job's suffering was horrific. And this led him to begin his speech in chapter 3, cursing the day of his birth.

Structure

For the most part, the structure of Job is easily recognizable. Job is bookended with narrative. Chapters one and two tell the story of how Job went from being a wealthy and blessed man to one who lost everything and was sitting in the ash pile, scraping himself with broken pottery to gain relief from his skin disease. Job 42:7–17 closes the story with the restoration of Job.

When you hear of the book of Job, most often it is from these narrative portions. Perhaps the best-known verse in the book is Job 1:21, "The LORD gave and the LORD has taken away. / Blessed be the name of the LORD."

To the reader's amazement, these words came from Job's mouth after he had lost everything, including his seven sons and three daughters.

Job 3 sets in motion the entire dialogue between Job and his friends. Job's three friends came from different locations to comfort him. After seven days and seven nights of sitting in silence with these friends, Job opened his mouth and said he wished he had never been born. In intricate poetry, Job cursed his own birthday, asking the key question, "Why is light given to him who suffers, / and life to the bitter of soul?" (Job 3:20).

If Job were destined for misery and suffering, then why was he born in the first place? This first chapter of the dialogue begins the debate between Job and his three friends. Three cycles of this dialogue go from chapter 3 through chapter 31.

Eliphaz spoke first, followed by Job's response. The next to speak was Bildad, followed by Job's response. Zophar then spoke, followed again by a response from Job. This cycle occurred three times. At the end of the third cycle, Bildad only gave a few sentences of argument. And Zophar did not even speak for the third cycle.

Job's final response to his friends actually began in chapter 26 and continued through chapter 31. But this is much less a response to his friends than a speech directed to God.

Interestingly, in chapter 32, a new character came on the scene. Elihu waited for the older friends to speak. But Elihu could stay silent no longer and broke out in chapter 32, ending his speech at the end of chapter 37. God then spoke to Job from chapters 38 through 41. Job responded to God in Job 42:1–6, which was followed by the concluding narrative.

Job 1–2	The narrative introduction of Job's suffering		
Job 3–27	The three cycles of debate		
		Job 3	Job's opening statement cursing his birthday
		Job 4–5	Eliphaz' first speech
		Job 6–7	Job's first response to Eliphaz
		Job 8	Bildad's first speech
		Job 9–10	Job's first response to Bildad
		Job 11	Zophar's first speech
		Job 12–14	Job's first response to Zophar
		Job 15	Eliphaz's second speech
		Job 16–17	Job's second response to Eliphaz
		Job 18	Bildad's second speech
		Job 19	Job's second response to Bildad
		Job 20	Zophar's second speech
		Job 21	Job's second response to Zophar
		Job 22	Eliphaz's third speech
		Job 23–24	Job's third response to Eliphaz
		Job 25	Bildad's third speech
		Job 26–27	Job's third response to Bildad
Job 28	Job's speech: Where is wisdom found?		
Job 29–31	Job's summary defense		
Job 32–37	Elihu's speech		
Job 38–41	God speaks to Job		
Job 42:1–6	Job responds to God		
Job 42:7–17	Job's restoration		

Themes

For the book of Job, it is best to speak first of the themes we see in the book before discussing the purpose of the book. This is because the more we study the book, the more we realize the purpose of the book has to be contextualized. It is not wise to give a one-sentence purpose statement for a book that deals with something as weighty as the problem of suffering.

Young Bible students and young theologians can tend to give quick answers. Even older Bible students can fall into the trap of oversimplifying. Job does give answers. The book does not sidestep the problem. But getting to the answers takes more than reading theology books and commentaries. The purpose of Job and its answers must simmer in life's pain for a while.

Suffering

A mutual understanding, and even a mutual affection, lies between those who have suffered great things. I used to think Job must have been the man who suffered the most. But the text does not make that claim. The text never says that Job suffered more than any other human in history.

Suffering is not only a common thread in all of human history, but in looking at the world's history. Even just looking at our own time, we see suffering is present more than it is absent.

Job was not unique in his suffering. Job was not the only one forced to bury his own children. Job was not the only one forced to endure a horrific illness. Job was not the only one whose friends turned on him in his intense suffering and his darkest hour.

Therefore, in approaching this book and attempting to understand its purpose, we must start with a sense of foreboding and gravitas. We cannot seek quick answers that are abstracted from reality. We must always keep in mind that everyone must grapple with the question of suffering and evil in the world. A span of millennia lies between us and Job. But in another sense, no span is between us at all because we all ask the same questions in light of our own suffering and the suffering we see around us.

The theme of suffering in Job is multilayered. The narrative tells us that Job lost all his children in the same day. In fact, Job was informed that he lost everything in the space of perhaps one minute. Job 1 tells the story of the messengers coming to Job to tell him the awful news.

The first messenger told Job that a raiding tribe took all of his oxen and donkeys. Before this messenger could get this sentence out of his mouth, the next messenger entered Job's presence to tell him that fire from God fell from heaven and burned up all of his sheep. Before this second messenger could get this sentence out of his mouth, the third one entered the scene to tell Job that all of his camels were stolen. Not only were his camels, oxen, and donkeys stolen and his sheep all burned up, but his servants who were with them were killed, except the three messengers.

The fourth messenger was with Job's children. He entered the scene to tell Job that the house where his children were feasting had collapsed, and everyone in the house was dead.

We see the suffering of Job in his physical illness. There was no medicine to alleviate the pain. Job was struck with an unknown illness described as being similar to smallpox. Job had no relief except to pick up pieces of broken pottery and scrape his skin.

We see the suffering of Job in his wife's response. Contrary to many others at this time in history, Job had only one wife. In the cultures of this era if a man were wealthy, he would often take multiple wives. Even the patriarch Jacob had two wives and two concubines.

Job had wealth. But Job had only one wife. Job also claims in the book that he was faithful to his wife, not even lustfully looking upon other women. We must also remember that Job's wife had also lost everything. She was only mentioned in two verses. Job 2:9 says Job's wife came to him and told him to just curse God and die. She told her faithful husband that he should just give up. At this point, Job had no one to comfort him at all.

We see Job's suffering with his friends. His three friends traveled a great distance to comfort him. Initially, the friends appeared as though they would be a great comfort to Job. When they saw him, they mourned with him, wept for him, and sat in silence with him for seven days and seven nights.

However, after Job opened his mouth in chapter 3, his friends quickly turned on him, telling him that while he looked like a righteous man outside, he must be a wicked man, and he must deserve what he received.

Eliphaz, even in his first speech, accused Job of being wicked and even said that the children of the wicked man are far from safety, and "They are even oppressed in the gate, / And there is no deliverer" (Job 5:4).

Job had just buried his children, who were crushed in the collapsed house, and Eliphaz basically told Job it was his fault because he must be evil.

We see suffering throughout the book. It is also multifaceted. Job not only suffered physically with illness, but he experienced gut-wrenching sorrow with the death of his children, the betrayal of his wife, and the reproach of his so-called friends.

Wisdom

We see the theme of wisdom in all of the Wisdom Literature books, and in many other portions of the Old Testament. However, as this is the first wisdom book that this survey is examining, it is important to examine the concept of wisdom from the outset.

Often, we view wisdom as something that is less significant than the Bible portrays it. We think of wisdom only in terms of skillful living. In this way we think of wisdom based on what it produces rather than on what it is. We think of wisdom in terms of making the right decisions and having insight into which direction to go.

In contrast, the American culture in the twenty-first century is defined by its quest for pleasure. The book of Job has a completely different worldview than this. Most Americans think the most comfortable life is the best life. It is the life lived in the context of wealth. It is being surrounded by the most exquisite food, the most beautiful things, and physical comfort. This pleasure-seeking worldview is completely different from Job's worldview.

It may sound shocking to say that Job's first priority in his suffering was not to get out of his physical suffering. That is not to say that Job was not looking for relief. But Job's first priority, as demonstrated throughout the book, was his desire to understand. Job wanted to comprehend what was happening and why.

Wisdom in the Old Testament involves comprehending everything that is going on around you and all that is happening to you according to that correct worldview. The quest for wisdom is the quest to comprehend correctly. It is a quest to understand the world and the events that surround us.

A fracture occurred in Job's worldview. Job never questioned God's sovereignty. Job and his friends held this presupposition and belief throughout the entire book. No one ever questioned whether God was in control.

The friends' argument was that Job suffered because of retribution. Job must have done some horrendous evil to bring about God punishing him for his wickedness.

In the eyes of Job's friends, the way to understand the world was through retribution. If you did good, God would bless you. If you did evil, God would punish you. Therefore, since Job was suffering, God must be punishing him, and therefore, Job must be wicked.

However, Job knew himself, and he knew he was a man of integrity. The author of the book described him that way, and even God described him the very same way.

Throughout the book, Job held fast to his integrity. He claimed innocence. Job did not claim to be perfect, but he did claim that he had not done some great evil which deserved this great suffering. Therefore, the fracture in Job's worldview was the conundrum of how a sovereign, all-powerful God could allow Job, a man of integrity, to suffer.

Job presupposed that God was sovereign. Job also believed God was good. Job believed that God hated evil. And Job's reality reminded him of his great suffering every second of the day. Job's priority in all of this was to comprehend why. Job wanted to understand how this could possibly be the case. This was Job's quest for wisdom. Wisdom was the tool Job used to seek to comprehend what was going on in the world and his circumstances.

The wisdom of the world would say there is no God, or at the very least, that God is not sovereign and does not care about what happens within our lives. Therefore, the wisdom of the world would say we should understand suffering in terms of bad luck.

You cannot explain suffering by the wisdom of the world. It happens to you, or it does not happen to you. And every human should try their hardest to avoid all suffering and to seek pleasure.

The wisdom of the world would say that we should pity those who are suffering, but ultimately there is no answer or reason for any suffering. Job did not base his thinking on the wisdom of the world. Job made a pivotal statement in Job 28:28. A variation of this statement is also mentioned in Proverbs and Ecclesiastes, along with Psalm 111. The statement in Job 28:28 is, "Behold, the fear of the LORD, that is wisdom; / And to depart from evil is understanding."

Proverbs adds the idea that the fear of God is the beginning of wisdom. If you want to comprehend correctly, to begin the journey of correctly understanding what goes on in the world and even what happens in your own life, you must begin with the fear of God.

The fear of God will come up in several chapters in this survey. But it is important to give a foundational understanding of the fear of God because of its centrality within the book of Job.

Perhaps the best way to describe the fear of God is to start by describing it as a recognition of our place before God. This is the Creator and creature distinction. It does away with the idea of diminishing God's sovereignty in order to account for suffering in the world.

We cannot explain suffering in the world by diminishing God's power, God's knowledge, or God's ability to intervene. Job consistently held to this position. If we want to be wise, if we want to truly comprehend, then according to Job, we must begin with the fear of God.

This fear of God, according to Job, is a right recognition of who God is and who we are. God is the Creator; we are the creatures. God has all power; we have no power. God is eternal; we are dust.

Recognizing that God is the Creator means we recognize that God is the authority, and God is the One who determines what is right. There is no higher law to appeal to than God Himself. God has ordered the universe in a particular way. Wisdom is the quest to understand what that order is. Therefore, wisdom must begin with a recognition of who God is.

The wisdom of the world will always fall short because the world does not recognize God nor honor him. But to say that God is all-powerful and sovereign is not enough, because the question of suffering remains. If God allows suffering or causes suffering, what does that tell us about His nature and His character?

Job 40:8 revealed one of God's questions to Job, "Will you condemn Me that you may be justified?"

While Job held fast to his integrity in the book, Job made several mistakes in the book. Job began to question God's character. He began to question whether God cared about him. God's answer came to him by way of several illustrations.

Natural Theology

If you read God's response to Job in chapters 38 through 41, you might be tempted to think God was not answering Job's question. Job wanted to understand why. Job wanted to comprehend and have a correct worldview that accounted for both God's sovereignty and the fact that Job was suffering.

God came on the scene and started to speak about His creation. God spoke about the storehouses of snow in the heavens. God spoke about the order of the stars. God spoke about an ostrich, a wild donkey, a warhorse, and many other creatures.

We might be tempted to think that God was sidestepping Job's question. But this is because we don't have a correct understanding of natural theology. The illustrations God used in His speech were intentional and specific.

The book of Job made no mention of the Mosaic Law or of any other scripture. Job and his friends gave examples of the way creation was ordered, and they extrapolated God's character from those observations. However, the friends didn't correctly account for how the universe was ordered. They had no place in their system for a righteous man who suffered. Job must have had a place in his system for a righteous man who was suffering because he knew he was righteous and was suffering.

The friends said many correct things about God. They didn't get everything wrong, but their system did not account for everything. Job threw their system of thinking aside in search of a new system that would explain to him how a righteous person could suffer. Job appealed to nature and to the organization of the world around him to explain what the Creator must be like. The friends did the same thing, though incorrectly.

When God came on the scene, He explained His own character through illustrations from His own creation. Every example God gave from the natural world was meant to highlight aspects of His character. God used the example of His own power in upholding and sustaining the world to remind Job of the Creator/creature distinction.

Job asked for his day in court with God as though he and God were on the same level, and God must be called to account. God reminded Job that He was the Creator and the authority. God cannot be called to account by any higher power.

Several of the illustrations God used pointed to His power, including the behemoth and leviathan. Behemoth was depicted as a real animal, something like a dinosaur. Leviathan was also described in physical terms, something akin to a dragon. God pointed to these two as pinnacles of His creation, saying humans had no ability to overpower or subdue these creatures. How much less did humans have ability to overpower, subdue, or even call to account the One who created these creatures.

God not only was putting Job in his place, He also gave illustrations from creation that spoke of His care for His creation. God asked who provided food for the animals. The fact that the lion had food to eat pointed to God's character as One who provides for His creation.

God pointed to the deer giving birth. Who took care of the deer with no human to witness? The order of God's creation pointed to His character not only as One who is almighty, but also One who is the provider, and One who upholds and cares for His creation.

God gave the example of the ostrich. God said He did not give the ostrich a share in understanding. The ostrich has no common sense. But God gave the ostrich exactly what it needs to survive: speed. The ostrich can outrun the horse and his rider. Though God did not give the ostrich great intelligence, He gave it exactly what it needed to do what God created it to do.

God was not sidestepping Job's questions. God was reminding Job of the order of creation set up in such a way to reflect the character of its Creator.

PURPOSE

God did not explain everything to Job. God did not tell Job about the scene in heaven in which He allowed Satan to go and cause great suffering to Job. God did not tell Job His reasons for allowing suffering. God did not tell Job that He must abide by a higher system that determines who suffers and who does not suffer.

God pointed to His authority and His sovereignty. God pointed to His character as a provider, as a sustainer, and as One who cares for His creation.

Job did not know why he had to suffer. As far as we know, Job never learned the specifics. Instead, God revealed Himself to Job, reminding him of His character.

Job reminds us that knowing the reasons for suffering are less necessary than the relationship between God and the one who is suffering. Those who suffer rarely get an answer in this life to their "why" question. Paul picked up on this in Romans 5:3–5, "We also exult in our tribulations, knowing that tribulation brings about perseverance; and perseverance, proven character; and proven character, hope; and hope does not disappoint, because the love of God has been poured out within our hearts through the Holy Spirit who was given to us."

Paul was not being flippant about suffering; he suffered a great deal in his earthly life. Paul also was not trying to dismiss physical suffering in exchange for some lofty, uninformed, spiritual theology. Paul was speaking of real suffering in the real world. He said we Christians can rejoice in our suffering because of what it produces within us, trusting that God will never leave us or forsake us. God's character remains the same. Even though we don't understand the reasons why, we trust in a God who is faithful, compassionate, and sovereign.

One additional thought I want to include in the discussion of the book of Job is the idea of beauty. Job 42 says God restored Job's fortunes. In fact, Job became twice as rich after his suffering than before.

We must read this portion carefully. The text is not saying that God replaced everything Job lost. We cannot read this narrative in terms of a worldview based on the pursuit of pleasure. It is not as though everything was now OK with Job because God gave him physical comfort again.

The suffering Job endured transformed the rest of his life. Job would never be the same again. He buried his own children. Although God gave him more children, that is not to say Job wasn't brokenhearted about the children he lost. Their names are not mentioned, but Job knew their names; Job loved them and had memories with them that no one else could replace.

The narrative in Job 42 is not meant to say that God replaced everything for Job. God did give Job great wealth again. And God gave him children again. But we should notice the emphasis placed upon Job's three daughters. Job's three daughters after his suffering are named in the text. Their names in Hebrew have to do with their beauty and their loveliness. In fact, the text says that in all the land, no women were so beautiful as Job's daughters. Their father gave them an inheritance among their brothers.

Job now better understood the value of life. God blessed Job by surrounding him with the gift of beauty. This was not the world's understanding of beauty, which is often distorted for the sake of self-gratification. This was a biblical understanding of beauty as a gift from God that points to His own beauty and goodness. It is an illustration within the creation to point us to the Creator, who kindly gives us pictures of beauty within the creation.

The purpose of Job is difficult to summarize in one sentence. Suffice it to say, Job's purpose is to explain how a sovereign, all-powerful, just, merciful, and loving God could have suffering within His creation, even in the lives of those who fear Him and love Him.

Wisdom begins with the fear of God, and wisdom is the tool by which we seek to understand how God has orchestrated creation and all human history for the good of His people and for His own glory.

Reflection questions:

1. How is someone who suffers better equipped to be a comfort to someone who is currently going through suffering?

2. What do you find to be most frustrating about Job's three friends? How can they say some correct things about God's character but still get so much wrong?

3. In what ways would you approach someone who is undergoing suffering in order to comfort them and also remind them of God's character?

4. In what way is beauty a relief or refreshment to those who are suffering?

2

Psalms

PSALMS IS CERTAINLY A pinnacle book in the Old Testament. It is a collection of psalms and praises to God as well as lamentations and many other forms of poetry. It was written over several centuries.

Psalm 90 is the earliest psalm whose author is known, a psalm of Moses. It is also argued that several of the psalms were written during the Exilic Period or even during the return from exile. From Moses until the return from the exile was roughly a millennium.

Besides the vast scope of time, the authors of the individual psalms were also quite varied. Many psalms do not give an author. Certainly, the one to whom the most psalms are attributed, is King David; 73 of the 150 psalms are attributed directly to him. Moses is only known to have written the one psalm. A person named Asaph wrote 12 psalms (Ps. 50, 73–83). Ten psalms are attributed to the sons of Korah (42, 44–49, 84, 85, 87). Two psalms are attributed to Solomon (72, 127). A man named Heman has one (88), and a man named Ethan has one (89).

Several of the psalms speak about musical accompaniment. A common introduction to an individual psalm is to say that it was written for "the choir master." An example would be Psalm 109.

Some psalms are given a particular musical title or musical category. Psalm 74 is specified as a *maskil*, which in Hebrew means it was to make the reader wiser or give the reader insight. Some musical terms are unclear today.

A notation that comes up from time to time in the psalms is the word *selah*. Some have argued that this Hebrew word is from a verb meaning to raise the voice higher. Others argue that it refers to a pause that should be taken in the music, something like an interlude.

Unfortunately, we do not know what all of these musical terms which are used in the psalms refer to. However, the psalms were meant to be sung, both individually and corporately.

Some psalms specify an intention. For example, Psalm 100 is titled as a psalm for giving thanks. Other psalms speak to the occasion of the writing.

For example, Psalm 63, a psalm of David, is noted as written when David was in the wilderness of Judah, still a lengthy period in his life. Some psalms are even more specific, such as Psalm 59, which was written when Saul sent men to watch David's house to kill him.

While some psalms give very specific history or intention or specific musical notation, other psalms have no such specificity. However, many Christians find it easy to relate to the psalms. The heart behind them, the anguish, the jubilation, or even the perplexity are readily seen within our own lives. In a way similar to that of the Wisdom Literature, the book of Psalms speaks about day-to-day living, human suffering, important life questions, and how we are to view and relate to God.

STRUCTURE

As already mentioned, the Psalms were written over an extensive period. There is some question as to when the book was compiled as we have it today. The book we have, which is 150 psalms, was certainly not completed in David's time, even though he was the main contributor. Whoever brought all the psalms together into the final, organized, 150 psalms we have seems to have arranged the psalms into five separate books:

Book 1: Psalms 1–41

Book 2: Psalms 42–72

Book 3: Psalms 73–89

Book 4: Psalms 90–106

Book 5: Psalms 107–150

Some of the transitions from book to book are also transitions of authorship. Book 1 includes, for the most part, the psalms of David. Psalm 42, which begins Book 2, is of the sons of Korah. The transition from Book 3 to Book 4 is Psalm 90, which was written by Moses. But the distinction in authorship is not a complete bifurcation of the books.

The five books appear to be divided to reflect the Pentateuch, the first five books of the Old Testament. Many scholars argue that these five books of the Psalms are meant to correspond to Genesis, Exodus, Leviticus, Numbers, and Deuteronomy. However, it can be difficult to take this down to the granular level for each of these psalms.

There are sections of the Psalms which designate a particular organization. Psalm 120 begins the Songs of Ascent, which carry all the way through

Psalm 134. The title of these psalms, "Songs of Ascent," may indicate that they were to be sung as pilgrims journeyed to Jerusalem, perhaps during the three annual feasts that required all Jewish males to be in Jerusalem.

It is also important to recognize Psalm 1 and Psalm 2 as introductory to the entire book. Psalm 1, a well-known psalm, speaks of the contrast between the man who follows after God and the wicked man. The righteous man is described as blessed, like a tree planted by streams of water. The wicked are in direct contrast, like chaff that the wind drives away.

This metaphor is seen throughout Psalms and elsewhere in the Old Testament. It describes the wicked as having no right place in the world. In contrast, the righteous have weight and honor and strong roots, like a tree. Much in the book of Psalms can be seen in this contrast between the righteous and the wicked.

Psalm 2 is a Messianic psalm, which is a central theme throughout Psalms. The Messiah is exalted and seen as a king who will end all rebellion. Jesus' last words on the cross before He died were even a quote from the first verse of Psalm 22, "My God, My God, why have You forsaken Me?"

The Psalms show extensive Messianic implications. In fact, the New Testament quotes from Psalms more than any other Old Testament book. The next most-quoted book in the New Testament is Isaiah. Deuteronomy plays a prominent role as well as Genesis and Exodus. But the fact that Psalms is the most quoted in the New Testament points to how well those in the New Testament times knew the book, and it also points to the vast extent to which the Psalms speak. Psalms 1 and 2 can be viewed as introductory psalms to the entire book, which set the stage for the rest of the book.

Purpose

Psalms speaks to a great many topics. But the fact that they are meant to be sung points to the central focus of the book in regard to worship. Worship is not to be understood as only singing to God in a happy manner. Instead, worship is all-encompassing, from the throes of deep darkness to the heights of exultation.

God was always the central focus of the psalms. Even when deep darkness surrounded the psalmists, they may have despaired for a time, but they turned to God for help in deliverance.

Psalm 23, the most well-known psalm, points to this reality. David declared that even though he walked in the valley of darkness, God was with him, leading him through the valley. Many different types of metaphors were used to show this reliance upon God. God was seen as a shepherd who took care of His sheep. God was seen as a strong tower into which the righteous ran and were safe. God was depicted as a rock. God was seen as a mighty warrior who fought on behalf of His people.

While many different metaphors were used, they all pointed to this central purpose, which was trust and reliance upon God. God's character was on display, whether in provision and protection of His beloved people or in punishment of the wicked.

All these psalms were set within real world contexts, so they dealt with problems such as the question of why the wicked seemed to prosper while the righteous suffered. But in all the psalms, God's character is on display, and God is trusted by the righteous one. This leads to reliance upon God and ultimately to worship of God in all situations of life.

> **PSALMS PURPOSE STATEMENT:** Even in the vicissitudes of life, God is to be worshipped because of His perfect character.

THEMES

God's Attributes

We could say God's attributes are a theme in every book of the Bible. That is a valid point. But especially within Psalms, God's attributes are described in intricate and specific ways. Worship comes about because of God's attributes, which are put on display.

Psalm 100 is a great example of this. This all begins with a command for all the earth to make a joyful noise to the Lord. The command is given to come into His presence with singing. Immediately after, the character of God is put on display. Verse 3 says that God is the Creator, that we belong to Him. Not only do we belong to Him, but He takes care of us like a shepherd does his sheep. Therefore, the psalm continues on with another command to give thanks to God and bless His name. There is another reiteration of God's character right after this. Verse 5 says God is good. Verse 5 also says God's steadfast love endures forever, and His faithfulness to all generations.

In five verses the psalmist has given commands for worship to be directed to God. The psalmist has put the character of God on display. God is shown to be all-powerful (as the Creator), caring (as the Shepherd), loving, faithful, and good. True worship is always informed by a correct understanding of God's character.

We can point to several different attributes of God that are most prominently on display within the psalms. We can see many different attributes of God throughout each of the psalms. Perhaps the most prominent of God's attributes is His love.

Unfortunately, in our day and age, the word "love" has lost its significance. The English word love is now used more to speak of someone's selfish desires. "True love" is depicted in the movies as something that is entirely satisfying and captivating.

In reality, when sin enters the equation, the beloved is no longer seen as being entirely captivating. In the world's definition of love, when problems come into the relationship, the relationship just ends as the participants search for someone else who will be captivating.

This is in direct contrast to God's love demonstrated within the Psalms. God's love demonstrates perfect loyalty. Psalm 107, which begins Book 5 in the Psalms, gives an excellent description of this loyal love. Verse 1 says God's steadfast, loyal love endures forever. Verse 2 commands the redeemed of the Lord to praise God because of this love. Verse 2 and following also describe those who are the beloved of God. The Psalm says that God redeemed them from trouble. God gathered them from all over the world. They were in great distress, as though wandering in a desert waste. They are depicted as prisoners in affliction and in darkness. Verse 17 says that some of them were like fools because of their sin.

Yet, God redeemed all of these beloved from their trouble. The reason for their redemption was not their own goodness, their own beauty, or their own character. God redeemed them and showed perfect loving loyalty to His people because of His own character. The psalms declare that because of this, we can trust and rely upon God. God's love is not determined on whether we perform in the right way or legalistically do the right thing. God's love is always and forever fixed upon His people, whom He chose. Therefore, nothing within us can cause God's love to be taken away from us.

Many more of God's attributes are on display in the Psalms. God's goodness is one of those key attributes. Psalm 25:8 says God is good and upright. Therefore, He instructs sinners in the way.

In other words, God's nature is one of goodness out of which only flows goodness. No perversity or corruption exists within God's nature. We know that God will always act according to His nature, and so He can be trusted.

Along with God's goodness, we see emphasis upon God's faithfulness. In contrast to humans, who say one thing and do another, God is always faithful to do exactly what He promises and to act in accordance with His good nature.

The outworking of God's goodness linked with God's faithfulness demonstrates God's righteousness. God's righteousness is the demonstration and outworking of His character. As in Psalm 145:7, the people sing aloud because of the righteous deeds God accomplishes on behalf of His people.

Messiah in the Psalms

In Matthew 22, Jesus silenced the Pharisees by asking them a simple question. Jesus quoted from Psalm 110 and asked the Pharisees how David could call the Messiah, who is descended from David, his Lord. Psalm 110, a psalm of David, begins with this statement, "The Lord says to my Lord: / 'Sit at My right hand / Until I make Your enemies a footstool for Your feet."

The Lord spoken of is the Messiah, and Psalm 110 says the Messiah will shatter kings on the day of His wrath and execute judgment among the nations. Interestingly, David, the author of this psalm, spoke about this Messiah who would be descended from David, and David called this Messiah his Lord. So, Jesus asked the Pharisees how David could call his own descendant his Lord. This Pharisees could not answer this simple question.

Throughout the Psalms, the Messiah is on display. The author of Hebrews used Psalm 110 in several places to expound upon the high priesthood of Jesus. Psalm 110:4 says the Messiah would be a priest forever according to the order of Melchizedek. This placed the Messiah's priesthood outside of the Aaronic priesthood. The Psalms give many other insights concerning the Messiah. The Messiah is consistently depicted as a king who was given all power to rule all the nations by God's own decree. The entire world, according to Psalm 2, is the inheritance that God gave to the coming Messiah.

Jesus quoted and applied Psalm 22 to himself on the cross. This psalm gives specific description of the suffering of the Messiah. Verse 6 says He is despised by the people. When Jesus quoted the first verse of this psalm from the cross, He showed its significance as a psalm that spoke about Him. Paired with the Prophets, Psalms portrays the Messiah both as a ruling king and conqueror, as well as One who suffers.

Imprecatory Psalms

The nature of imprecatory psalms is an often questioned. The question often involves whether this is something that Christians should do regularly. Imprecatory psalms are prayers that ask God for destruction of the wicked.

In many instances David and other psalmists asked God to destroy the wicked. This is seen in descriptive ways, such as God trampling the wicked into the dust. Some of these psalms do not speak generally but are specific to a particular context in which the psalmist asks for destruction upon a particular enemy.

The enemy is described as one who hates God, one who is in full rebellion against God. The psalmist points to his own character saying that he fears God and follows the commandments of God. The psalmist also at times does not see a clear way of escape from his enemies. It appears his enemies surround him and are ready to destroy him. The psalmist's only hope is for God to deliver by destroying his enemies.

While many of the psalms are easily relatable, it can be difficult to understand and apply these psalms in our own lives. While these psalms should not be discounted, it is important to see them in light of salvation coming to both the Jews and the Gentiles. In several places in the Psalms, the gospel going to all the nations is put on display.

Psalms 33 and 67 are good examples of the gospel going to the entire world. Israel was never meant to be the only nation that followed God. The people of God were never to be only those within ethnic Israel.

While a clear contrast is made between the righteous and the wicked, at several points within Psalms, we see the intention and the desire for all of the world and all of the nations of the earth to follow God. Psalm 33:8 says, "Let all the earth fear the LORD; / Let all the inhabitants of the world stand in awe of Him!"

Verse 18 says the eye of the Lord is on those who fear Him, that He might deliver them. Those who fear Him should come from all of the nations. Psalm 33:12 is that well known verse, "Blessed is the nation whose God is the LORD."

Psalm 67 is even more specific about the gospel going to all the nations. Verse 1 asks that God would be gracious to Israel and bless Israel so God's way may be known on earth and God's saving power known among all nations. Verse 3 says all people should praise God; let the nations be glad and sing for joy. Psalms points to both Jew and Gentile who would fear God, trusting in God's attributes that they might be saved. But those who would reject God, those who hate God, they were to be judged.

The New Testament emphasizes turning the other cheek. While God will fully and finally destroy the wicked as well as save the righteous, the New Testament gives a particular role to the Christian. The Christian is not to seek his or her own retribution. The Christian is to trust and rely upon the vengeance of the Lord.

Reflection questions:

1. Why do you think that Christians often find the Psalms the most relatable of all the sections of the Old Testament?
2. Why is the theme of the Messiah such a central focal point for the Psalms? How does this relate to the character of God being displayed throughout the Psalms? How does this relate to worship being the central purpose?
3. What do imprecatory psalms teach us about God's character? Should these psalms be emulated by Christians today? Why or why not?
4. In what way are Psalms 1 and 2 an introduction to the entire book of Psalms?

3

Proverbs

PROVERBS IS A BOOK FOR young people. Its primary audience is the people who lack wisdom and discernment. But the book of Proverbs also has timeless truths that are to be mulled over throughout one's life.

No one will ever master the book of Proverbs, just like no one can master any of the Wisdom Literature. As life progresses, we see things from new perspectives because of the events that come into our lives. The way we read a proverb when we are young will change and be deepened when we read that same proverb as an old person. The quest for wisdom is never completed in this life.

Solomon wrote this book to his young son, encouraging him again and again to pursue wisdom and seek understanding while he was young. Rather than learn the hard way through experience, Solomon directed his son to avoid pitfalls and wickedness, which bring devastation. Young people often do not know how decisions in their youth will affect the rest of their lives.

The book of Proverbs must be taken on faith. Some young people are more apt to listen and trust than others. Those who seek to learn things on their own often repeat the same mistakes their parents made. Parents have the obligation to take what they have learned and apply it to their children to help their children avoid foolishness.

Even though these proverbs were written millennia ago, they are directly applicable to life in the twenty-first century. Those who ignore this wisdom are doomed to make the mistakes Proverbs warned about.

Solomon's life was characterized by mistakes. Solomon warned his son not to be seduced by wayward women, but Solomon was led astray by wicked women. Solomon brought an interesting perspective in that he was foolish enough to make horrible mistakes, and he was wise enough to repent and seek to train the next generation to be more disciplined and more faithful than he was.

Unfortunately, when we look into Israel's history, we see that Solomon's son Rehoboam, who succeeded him as king, was characterized by foolishness.

He followed the advice of his foolish friends, leading to the division of the kingdom and even to civil war. We should learn a lesson from this and seek to pursue this wisdom throughout our lives, especially when we are young.

STRUCTURE

The structure of Proverbs is notoriously difficult to pin down. We can see several elements of structure throughout the book, but it is difficult to determine the overall structure of the entire book.

The book begins with a clear purpose and introduction in the first seven verses. In fact, Solomon began the book in a fascinating way. For the first six verses, Solomon used few verbs. Instead, he gave several different infinitives that speak to the purpose of the book.

We can see this when he said things such as in verse 2, "To know wisdom and instruction, / To discern the sayings of understanding." This is not a grammatically complete sentence, but these statements point to Solomon's intention in writing his proverbs.

We can see the thesis statements of the book in chapter 1, verse 7, "The fear of the LORD is the beginning of knowledge; / Fools despise wisdom and instruction."

This statement is in all the other Wisdom Literature books in the Old Testament. We have already seen this in Job 28:28 and will see it again in Ecclesiastes in several instances.

Solomon was writing to his son, who was unnamed. Proverbs 1:8 told the son that he should pay attention to his father's instruction and to his mother's teaching.

This command to seek wisdom is seen in many places in Proverbs. The beginning of each chapter gives a new admonition for the young man to listen to his father's instruction. This goes all the way through chapter 7 in which Solomon told his son to obey his words and treasure his commands.

Chapters 1 through 7 were clearly directed to Solomon's son, and the sections can be broken down by different themes. The theme to avoid the adulteress comes up in many instances. Solomon also spent time telling his son to avoid laziness and to avoid wicked friends.

In chapters 8 and 9, a comparison was made between Lady Wisdom and Lady Foolishness. Both were calling out and telling people to follow them. Lady Wisdom's path would lead to life while Lady Foolishness would lead to death (Prov. 9:18). Proverbs 9:10 gives another statement that the fear of the Lord is the beginning of wisdom.

Chapter 10 through Proverbs 22:16 is a collection of proverbs, and at times their organization can be difficult to see. Often, it is best to take each one on its own, one verse at a time. Each is meant to prompt critical thinking about how to correctly interpret the world and how to correctly act.

Proverbs 22:17 begins an additional section that is described as the words of the wise. It is probably best to see this section, which goes all the way through the end of chapter 24, as proverbs written by several different wise people.

Chapter 25 begins with a statement that these are proverbs of Solomon. This section goes all the way through the end of chapter 29. We then see the Proverbs of Agur in chapter 30. Lemuel had his own proverbs in 31:1–9 as well as his discussion of the "excellent wife" in 31:10–31. This is commonly known as the Proverbs 31 woman, and this ends the book.

Proverbs 1:1	Title
Proverbs 1:2–6	Introduction
Proverbs 1:7	The fear of the Lord
Proverbs 1:8–7:27	A father's instruction to his son
Proverbs 8–9	Lady Wisdom and Lady Foolishness
Proverbs 10:1–22:16	The proverbs of Solomon
Proverbs 22:17–24:34	The proverbs of the wise
Proverbs 25–29	Additional proverbs of Solomon
Proverbs 30	The proverbs of Agur
Proverbs 31:1–9	The proverbs of Lemuel
Proverbs 31:10–31	The excellent wife

Purpose

The introduction of Proverbs clearly shows its purpose. Solomon laid out the claim that he desired the book to instruct youth, especially his son, in wisdom. The point of the book is that the worldview of the young and the naive might be shaped to understand how God has orchestrated the world and the principles by which we should live.

If we understand the purpose of Proverbs correctly, we will not fall into the trap of thinking that everything written in Proverbs is a promise without exception. Some of the Proverbs are truisms. An example would be Proverbs 10:23, which says shameful conduct is a pleasure for a fool. This is true by definition because, in order to be a fool, you would take pleasure in wicked and shameful conduct, according to Proverbs.

However, some proverbs point to the ideal. Proverbs 12:13 says an evil man is trapped by his rebellious speech, but a righteous person escapes from trouble. Unfortunately, this is not always the case in the world. Sometimes an evil man gets away with rebellious speech. And sometimes a righteous person does not escape from trouble.

Another example commonly given is Proverbs 22:6, which says that if you train a child in the way he should go, when he is old, he will not depart from it. Proverbs is not promising that every parent who trains a child in godliness will always have children who follow God. While this is often the case because of God's blessing, this is not a promise with no exceptions.

We must be careful to understand the purpose of Proverbs, which is to point to the ideal world, to point to how God has created the world and the rules and principles by which the world operates. Because of God's character, the way He has created the world would yield a righteous man having wealth and long life. Solomon says that based on the principles set forth in the creation and the way God has orchestrated the world, if you are wise and righteous then you will be wealthy, and you will have a long life, and you will have a wonderful marriage, and you will have godly children.

The problem is that we don't live in a perfect world. Proverbs points to the ideal and shows what should be the case. The wicked should be destroyed and brought to ruin. The righteous should flourish. But as we look at the world around us, we see that often the righteous do not flourish, but rather the wicked are placed in prominent positions and have wealth.

This is why we must read all of the Wisdom Literature together. In a sense, we start with Proverbs, and we learn about the ideal, about how the fear of God brings about prosperity and blessing. But we cannot fall into the trap of Job's friends, thinking that this system can be manipulated.

Job's friends viewed the organization of God's creation and the principles by which it runs as something of a machine. If you put in the fear of God and you put in righteous deeds, then out comes long life, material blessing, and good health. The book of Job compliments the book of Proverbs well in showing what the response of someone who is righteous should be in the face of suffering, when things do not go the way that you expect them to.

Ecclesiastes should also be understood within this group. Solomon, in Ecclesiastes, at the end of his life, pointed to how sin affects the world. In Ecclesiastes, he pointed to the vanity of living in a system corrupted by sin.

So, each of the Wisdom Literature books should be understood in relationship to the other, not in isolation. If we isolate each of these books, then our perspective and our worldview will be skewed. Proverbs is the most principle-based, showing how God has established principles to live by. But we must also consider that God's ways are not our ways and God's thoughts are not our thoughts. We should live according to the fear of the Lord because we love God, not because we seek to gain material wealth or physical blessing.

> **Proverbs Purpose Statement:** The fear of the Lord is the beginning of wisdom, which leads to living God's way.

Themes

Proverbs contains many different themes. A person would be able to compile each of the individual Proverbs into groups that speak about similar themes. I will delve into a few of these most prominent themes.

Lady Wisdom and Lady Folly

A key theme and contrast made throughout Proverbs is that between Lady Wisdom and Lady Folly. We clearly see this in Proverbs 8 and 9, but it is throughout many portions of the book.

One of the first things that Solomon warned his son about was the seductive woman. Chapter 5 is a lengthy portion commanding the reader to be faithful to the wife of his youth. The idea was that Solomon's son would be married to one woman in his youth, and that he would be faithful to that woman throughout his entire life.

Solomon warned his son that the Lord sees everything (5:21). Solomon gives a positive command that his son should take pleasure in the wife of his youth, finding satisfaction with her alone. In contrast to this is the fool who captivated by the seduction of the wicked woman and follows after her like a lamb to the slaughter.

Solomon warned that though the lips of the forbidden woman drip honey, in the end, she only gives bitterness. Her feet go down to death, and she doesn't even understand the path of life. Solomon warned his son to keep far away from her, not even going near the door of her house.

This picture is taken even further in Proverbs to speak about the juxtaposition of Lady Wisdom and Lady Folly. Chapters 8 and 9 make this clear comparison. Lady Wisdom calls out and tells anyone who will listen to her that she speaks the truth and that she leads to life. Lady Wisdom says that she was there when God established the heavens, when He created the world. Through wisdom, God created the universe. And wisdom calls out for everyone to follow.

Lady Folly also calls out to anyone who will listen. Lady Folly seduces and tells the foolish and the ignorant that she will give them great pleasure and satisfaction. But Solomon said that those who go after her don't even know they are on the path of death.

This theme is also seen practically in the Proverbs 31 woman. This woman is characterized by goodness, faithfulness, wisdom, and security. In fact, Proverbs 31:10–31 is a chiasm with a central focus on the good name that this wife brings for her husband.

A High value of a good wife (10)
  B Husband benefited by wife (11–12)
    C Wife works hard (13–19)
      D Wife gives to the poor (20)
        E No fear of snow (21a)
          F Children clothed in scarlet (21b)
            G Coverings for bed, wife wears linen (22)
              H Public respect for husband (23)
            G' Sells garments and sashes (24)
          F' Wife clothed in dignity (25a)
        E' No fear of future (25b)
      D' Wife speaks of wisdom (26)
    C' Wife works hard (27)
  B' Husband and children praise wife (28–29)
A' High value of a good wife (30–31)

In stark contrast to the Proverbs 31 woman is the foolish woman who is depicted as being an exhaustion to her husband. Solomon said it is better to live on the corner of your roof than in the house with a contentious and quarrelsome wife.

One of the best things Solomon said his son could do was to find a godly wife and be faithful to her throughout his entire life. This would bring great blessings, joy, and life. Proverbs 19:14 is a beautiful statement, "House and wealth are an inheritance from fathers, / But a prudent wife is from the LORD." While one may become rich because of the hard work of one's parents, finding a godly wife is a gift from God that cannot be inherited like wealth is.

Diligence vs. Laziness

While many themes can be discussed within Proverbs, one of the most prominent is the contrast between diligence and laziness. Solomon told the lazy person to go look at the ant in order to learn from the ant's diligence and hard work.

Solomon described a lazy person as not plowing or doing any work during planting season, and when harvest time comes, he expected to have food and produce, but of course there was nothing (20:4). The one who is lazy is akin to a vandal (18:9).

Solomon painted a vivid picture when he said the lazy one would bury his hand in the bowl, but he was so lazy he didn't even bring his hand back to his mouth (19:24). In contrast, the diligent person's work would bring honor.

Wisdom brings correct understanding of how the world works. And this leads to diligence in work, forward thinking, and preparation. The lazy were depicted as only looking at what was right in front of them to their own hurt and destruction.

Godly Speech

An additional theme we should emphasize is the idea of speech. Throughout Proverbs, much is said about speaking with wisdom. Proverbs 15:1 says a gentle answer turns away anger, but a harsh word stirs up wrath. Right after this, Solomon said that the tongue that heals is a tree of life but a devious tongue breaks the spirit.

Proverbs 18:2 says that a fool does not delight in understanding but only wants to show off his opinions. The fool is depicted as one who uses words to manipulate and to boast. The wise one understands the value of words and seeks to communicate the truth. Words can bring favor, grace, and refreshment. Words also can bring pain, disgrace, and heartache.

Along with this idea is Solomon's teaching about listening. Not only is it important to speak in a godly way, but a person should also be quick to listen in order to learn. Proverbs 19:20 says that a person should listen to counsel and receive instruction in order to be wise later in life. Fools are quick to multiply words. Those who are wise are quick to listen.

Reflection questions:

1. What other themes do you see in the book of Proverbs? What does Proverbs have to say about God's sovereignty? What about the role of the king?
2. Why is wisdom so necessary early in life? Why do you think it is rare for young people in today's culture to pursue wisdom?
3. How do Solomon's mistakes give clarity to the book of Proverbs? Is Solomon just being hypocritical? Why do you think Solomon finds it so necessary to direct this book to his son?

4

Ecclesiastes

ECCLESIASTES IS INCLUDED in the Wisdom Literature books of the Old Testament, which include the Proverbs as well as Job. The author of Job is unknown. The book does not reveal the author. Scholars have made different suggestions and arguments, but nothing is final.

The book of Proverbs makes several claims of authorship. They're the sayings of Lemuel, Agur, and others. Solomon is the primary contributor to Proverbs. For Ecclesiastes, the author has been debated. Some scholars say it is someone pretending to be Solomon. Some argue that it is not possible to know who the author of Ecclesiastes is.

However, the text makes a clear assertion as to its own authorship. The book begins with the statement, "The words of the preacher, the son of David, king in Jerusalem."

The author does not name himself in the first verse but claims to be a son of David and also king in Jerusalem. In Hebrew, the word "son," similar to English, can mean either the direct son or a descendant. More specificity is given in 1:12, where the preacher says he is king over Israel in Jerusalem.

The only son of David who was king over all of Israel, and not just over Judah, was Solomon. Though Solomon did not name himself, he did claim to be the author of the book. This claim should be taken at face value, clearly showing that Solomon is the author of Ecclesiastes.

It is interesting that Solomon did not name himself but gave himself the title *Qoheleth*. This Hebrew word, often translated into English as "preacher," gives the idea of someone who presides over an assembly. *Qoheleth* is the one speaking to the group, trying to help them understand the nature of wisdom and the nature of this present life.

In Proverbs, Solomon clearly indicated why he was writing. He said the book was written to make the naive and simple wise. The book was written to teach wisdom to those who feared and loved God. Solomon did not have this same kind of purpose statement at the beginning of Ecclesiastes, but he set up the book in a unique way that demonstrated why he was writing it.

Solomon began the book by repeating the Hebrew word for vanity: *hevel*. This word had several different connotations. What is striking in chapter 1 is that Solomon placed everything into the category of vanity. He said that everything, without exception, in this created world, is in the category of being *hevel*. Ecclesiastes 1:3–11 expounded on this idea.

Solomon described everything as being cyclical with no end in sight. He said all things are wearisome, man is not able to tell it. Humans are never satisfied with seeing or hearing, and nothing was new under the sun. Not only that, but there's no remembrance of things that pass away. We will say more about this in the section on the themes of Ecclesiastes. It is important to see the distinction between Ecclesiastes, Job, and Proverbs.

Proverbs sets forth the ideals of life. Proverbs claims that if you are wise and fear God, then the natural outcome would be that you are wealthy, and you will have long life. Proverbs points to the ideals and the way God created the world to work. Even in a world that includes sin and wickedness, those who are the enemies of God should perish while those who are righteous flourish. Proverbs points to the way things should be.

In juxtaposition to this are the books of Job and Ecclesiastes. All students of the Bible recognize that the book of Job deals with the problem of suffering. Why do bad things happen to good people, those who fear God and have integrity?

Ecclesiastes comes at the issue from a different vantage point. Ecclesiastes does not necessarily focus on the issue of suffering, which is external to the person. Instead, the focus is on the futility of life. Ecclesiastes asked the question, "Why does anything matter?" Ecclesiastes 1:13 says, "*It* is a grievous task *which* God has given to the sons of men to be afflicted with."

This statement is related to the question Job asked in Job 3:20, "Why is light given to him who suffers?" If Job asks why there is suffering, then Ecclesiastes asks the question of why is there futility.

STRUCTURE

The structure of Ecclesiastes also points to the purpose and intention behind the book. Even when we contrast Job, Proverbs, and Ecclesiastes, we see a clear distinction between the structures of these books. Job, Proverbs, and Ecclesiastes all feature the fear of God as a central theme. However, Proverbs begins with the statement that the fear of God is the beginning of wisdom (Prov. 1:7). This statement occurs in the mid portion of Job at a key time in the book (Job 28:28). Within Ecclesiastes, the fear of God is the focus of the middle portion and the end. Solomon made a key statement in Ecclesiastes 12:13, "The conclusion, when all has been heard, *is*: fear God and keep his commandments, because this *applies* to every person."

The fear of God is the central focus of each of these books. But each book approaches this idea from a different perspective. We might even say the Proverbs is deductive, beginning with the thesis statement of the fear of God. Proverbs begins with this idea and then expounds on what this looks like as an ideal.

In contrast, Ecclesiastes begins with the problem and asks what the solution would be, closing the argument of the book with the answer of the fear of God. In this way, we might say Ecclesiastes is inductive, beginning with all the examples of problems leading to the conclusion and the thesis statement.

Some scholars argue that Ecclesiastes is a chiasm. The book begins and ends with the author mentioned in the third person. Chapters 1 and 11 discuss the brevity of life. Chapter 3 and chapter 7 include poems about time. Chapter 4 and chapter 5:13–20 speak about suffering. Ecclesiastes 4:7–16 and 5:8–17 discuss the problem of people who are obsessed with gaining wealth. This puts the central focus on Ecclesiastes 5:1–7, which teaches the fear of God.

Solomon warns the readers to guard their steps when they go to the house of God. It is better to obey than to offer the sacrifice of fools. Solomon warns the readers not to be hasty to speak but to be silent and reverent before God. The conclusion of verse 7 is simple: Fear God.

PURPOSE

We have already mentioned the centrality of the fear of God. But what did Solomon mean by the fear of God? Did he mean we are to live in dread of Him? Solomon had not given up on life. Solomon sought to understand the purpose of life and the reason why life seems futile.

The important phrase that recurs in Ecclesiastes is "under the sun." This phrase is a metaphor that intentionally points to the place of humans in creation. This phrase emphasizes the cyclical patterns of creation. Chapter 1 even speaks about the sun as constantly rising and setting. The circuit of the sun seems to have no end.

Similarly, there seems to be no end to the striving and labor of humans. At the beginning of the book, Solomon asked the key question of what a person gains for all this toil under the sun. It appears people work hard to make money to buy food so they have the strength to keep working hard.

Solomon spoke in the same way about pleasure. He used himself as an example of one who sought all kinds of pleasures. Solomon was incredibly wealthy and powerful. In Ecclesiastes 2:10 he said he did not deny his eyes anything they wanted. He came to the end of this pleasure and realized that this also was futile, not granting true satisfaction, and still bound up within the system of being under the sun.

So Solomon asked, "What does pleasure accomplish. What does toil accomplish?" Solomon pointed to some good things. He said it is better to be wise than to be foolish, but even wisdom leads to heartache because you see the futility of life.

In chapter 4, Solomon said two are better than one. It is a good thing to have a companion. But the problem Solomon kept encountering was the fact that everything and everyone dies. He said a living dog was better than a dead lion. But everything dies, so what is the point?

Solomon was describing the system of living under the sun. We might think of this in terms of the world's philosophy. Those who deny God, if they're intellectually honest, must admit that nothing truly matters.

In contrast to this worldly philosophy, the argument of Solomon was that those who fear God must live in light of the end of their lives. They should live in such a way that they see the good things of this life as gifts from God, not as something that they are entitled to.

> **ECCLESIASTES PURPOSE STATEMENT:** In contrast to only living "under the sun," those who fear God should live in light of the end, enjoying life as a gift, not the end in and of itself.

THEMES

As with all the Wisdom Literature books, we can examine many themes within Ecclesiastes. A few will be highlighted below. It is important to see the relationship between Ecclesiastes and Genesis.

Solomon, in the way he described his accomplishments and work, clearly wanted us to think about Genesis and about humanity's fall into sin in Genesis and the repercussions that come from that. In addition to this, we will examine the concept of futility and accomplishment.

In Ecclesiastes, Solomon examined the idea of the labor and hard work people put into this life without thinking about their impending death. Time marches on with no one to stop it. Finally, we will examine the good things Solomon spoke about, the blessings God has given.

Ecclesiastes and Genesis

In several places in Ecclesiastes, Solomon clearly made connection to the early chapters of Genesis. In Ecclesiastes 3:20, Solomon said that all come from dust and all return to dust. Right after the fall, God reminded Adam that he would eat food by the sweat of his brow until he returned to the ground, since he was taken from it. "For you are dust, / And to dust you shall return" (Gen. 3:19).

Perhaps the place most clearly tied to Genesis is Ecclesiastes 2. Solomon described aspects of his building projects in creation terms, with description similar to the Garden of Eden. Solomon had fantastic wealth and the ability and opportunity to undertake massive construction projects. Solomon said he made gardens and parks (the English word "Paradise" comes from this Hebrew word) for himself. In these gardens he planted "every kind of fruit tree." This points back to God's creation of the Garden of Eden, in which God planted all kinds of fruit trees.

With the same structure as we see in the creation account, Solomon spoke about the water sources he brought into these gardens. Genesis 2 speaks about the river that flowed through the Garden of Eden and afterward divided into four separate rivers.

Solomon spoke about the gold he had, also mentioned in Genesis 2 (the gold of Havila). Solomon described his building projects as an attempt to get back to Eden, or perhaps to try to replicate Eden. However, Solomon came to the end of these building projects and said, "Thus I considered all my activities which my hands had done and the labor which I had exerted, and behold all was vanity and striving after wind and there was no profit under the sun" (Eccl. 2:11).

No matter how hard Solomon tried, he couldn't return to Eden. He couldn't extricate himself from a life lived under the sun. We can understand the phrase "under the sun" as a parallel idea with living post-Eden.

In Genesis 3 right after the fall, God pronounced the curse. Because of humans' fall into sin, the ground was cursed, producing thorns and thistles. The ground no longer did exactly what it was created to do.

When God created the world, He pronounced everything as good. He blessed the world, emphasizing that everything in the world did exactly what He created it to do. The fish, birds, animals, and humans were good because they did exactly what God created them to do.

When sin enters the world, a breakdown happens. Things no longer work right. The ground no longer does exactly what it was created to do.

Animals started eating each other. Deception and maliciousness now existed. A fracturing took place in human relationships. Ultimately, a fracturing occurred in the relationship between man and God.

In Genesis 3 God pronounced the curse in stark contrast to the blessing we see in Genesis 1–2. Solomon wanted that blessing from Genesis 1–2. The book of Proverbs points to this blessing, claiming that in the ideal world, if a person is righteous and does what God created that person to do, then that person experiences blessing. But in Ecclesiastes, Solomon pointed out that the blessing is broken. Ecclesiastes 1:15 says, "What is crooked cannot be straightened."

In other words, there is no way to rewind the clock. Everything now is tainted with futility and emptiness and brokenness. This includes physical problems, such as the breakdown of the human body in the aging process. This includes social problems, with the fracturing of relationships and the lack of trust because of sin. This includes spiritual problems, with the ultimate question of how a person is supposed to relate to his or her Creator.

Futility, Death, and the Movement of Time

Besides this theme of the contrast between Genesis and Ecclesiastes, we see the theme of the march of time. Everything is tainted with futility. And every living thing will die.

Ecclesiastes 3 is a central passage that speaks about time. Solomon said there is a time for everything. He then spent seven verses listing opposites. There is a time to weep and a time to laugh. There's a time to kill and a time to heal. There is a time to plant and a time to uproot. There is a time to keep and a time to throw away. There is a time for war and a time for peace.

At first glance we wonder why Solomon listed these things. He explained his intention in verses 9 to 15. He asked the same question in verse 9 that he asked at the beginning of the book: What does the worker gain from his toil?

Solomon explained that God gave people a task to be occupied with. God has given people work to be done. For instance, if you want to eat, you need to plant food. So not only does the world appear to be cyclical and futile, but God was the one who gave humans the tasks they were to be consumed with.

In 3:11 Solomon added, "He has also set eternity in their heart, yet so that man will not find out the work which God has done from the beginning even to the end."

As with Proverbs and Job, Ecclesiastes presumes that God is sovereign. Not only is there a time for all these things, but God has appointed the times. In addition to this, God has put eternity into the heart of man.

Solomon meant that people are able to think past their own lifetimes. This separates humans from animals, which have no ability to think past their life spans. Humans look at history and look to the future, not asking questions about what God is doing from the beginning to the end. However, humans are not able to understand this perfectly.

Ecclesiastes 3:14 says that God has established it this way so that people will fear Him. God has set it up this way so all people recognize that He is the Creator, and we are the creatures. We are dependent upon Him, not the other way around. We are finite, and God is infinite. God sovereignly controls the times and directs history.

In a similar way to what we find in the book of Job, humans are meant to understand God's character from how He has orchestrated the world. From the perspective of humans, time seems to march on with no end. However, God knows the beginning and the end and is sovereign over all of it.

Even though a person does not know exactly what will happen to him or her after death, God does. Therefore, humans are to live in light of the end. In fact, this is exactly how Solomon ended the book of Ecclesiastes, saying, "For God will bring every act to judgment, everything which is hidden, whether it is good or evil" (Eccl. 12:13). All will be brought to account; therefore humans are to fear God.

The Gifts of God

Not everything within Ecclesiastes is bleak. Again, Solomon had not given up on life. Solomon was using wisdom to understand the nature of life. He wanted to understand how God created the world and to live according to the principles that God set forth.

Anyone who tries to live outside of those principles is only harming himself or herself and pursuing futility. Solomon gave the metaphor of someone chasing after the wind. There is nothing to be gained, and no goal that will ultimately be accomplished.

Solomon also pointed to the good gifts God gives to people. God is not a tyrant. God is not vindictive. God does not seek to harm His people. God's character is on display in the way He blesses His people even in a system marred by wickedness.

The blessing God gives to fallen humanity is a sign of a full redemption to come. There is hope that God will fully and finally bring His people out of this system of futility. And even within with this evil world, God grants blessing and joy and satisfaction to His people.

In chapter 11 Solomon spoke about business ventures. He gave the often-used verse of casting your bread on the waters, for after many days you will find it. The idea is that we should take some level of risk and seek to accomplish many things within our lifetimes.

Solomon said we do not know how things will ultimately turn out in our lives, but that should not cause us to stop working. In 11:6, Solomon said we are to sow our seed and work hard because we do not know how we will succeed. Solomon said that God gives us light, which is sweet and pleasing to the eyes. In verse 8 Solomon said, "Indeed, if a man should live many years, let him rejoice in them all, and let him remember the days of darkness, for they will be many."

Humans are always to live with the understanding that the world is full of suffering. But we are also to rejoice in the gifts God gives, including life, wealth, good friends, a true companion, and many other things. Solomon commanded his readers to remove sorrow from their hearts and put away pain from their flesh (Eccl. 11:10).

Solomon was not saying we should seek as much pleasure as we can but to live in light of the end. This is a true recognition of the effects of sin in the world and the devastation that comes from rebelling against God. But it is also a recognition of our loving God who gives us good gifts, pointing to the perfect gift of redemption in Christ Jesus.

Reflection questions:

1. How are the books of Ecclesiastes, Proverbs, and Job different in how they teach wisdom and how they make use of the fear of God in their arguments?

2. How would you explain Solomon's use of the phrase "under the sun"?

3. How does Ecclesiastes contrast youth with old age? How is this a book for both the young and the old?

4. How does Solomon speak about work ethic and how a person should approach work as a follower of God?

5

Song of Solomon

UNFORTUNATELY, THIS book is not often preached in pulpits. As we will discuss in the purpose section, there are some differences in how the book is interpreted, whether literally or allegorically. Song of Solomon speaks to the beauty, intimacy, and joy of a God-honoring relationship between a man and his bride.

The book speaks of Solomon as being king at the time of its writing. It is best to place the date of writing within the period of Solomon's reign, perhaps even in the early portion of his reign as king. Solomon began ruling in 970 BC and died in 931 BC.

The first verse of the book gives the title and also speaks about Solomon, "The Song of Songs, which is Solomon's." This statement about Solomon can be taken in a few different ways. It may be said that this is a book concerning Solomon, making Solomon the groom. A person could also read this as a book authored by Solomon.

The unfolding of the book follows the story of the lover and the beloved. There is an initial interaction and desire for each other. A courtship follows. Song of Solomon 3:6–11 describes Solomon arriving for his own wedding. This is followed by a description of the intimacy between the bride and groom, which is followed by a separation of the bride from her husband. They are reunited and speak of their longing and love for each other.

The beloved, who becomes the bride, is described throughout the book. Chapter 1 says she is dark of skin and lovely and describes her as a shepherdess. She was no stranger to hard work, speaking about growing up working with her brothers. In the eyes of the groom, she is the most beautiful among women (1:8). She reciprocates these praises and speaks of the groom's strength and beauty. We see their physical desire for each other throughout the book, as well as their emotional and spiritual bond.

We also see other characters in the book— a group of friends who speak. They speak only occasionally and celebrate the love that is witnessed in several of the stages of the relationship.

STRUCTURE

Noting keywords and repetition used throughout Song of Solomon is the key to seeing the structure. The eight chapters which compose the book are a chiasm. The first verse is given as a title. The beloved begins to speak right after this starting in verse 2. From verse 2 all the way into the final verse, we see the focus into the heart of the book. We can see the chiasm in the following breakdown:

- A Come away together (1:2–4a)
  - B Friends (1:4b)
    - C "My own vineyard" (1:5–7)
      - D Description of the beloved (1:8–14)
        - E "House" (1:15–2:2)
          - F "His left hand" (2:3–7)
            - G Fragrance and blossoming (2:8–13)
              - H "Vineyards" (2:14–15)
                - I "My beloved is mine" (2:16–17)
                  - Ja "The watchmen found me" (3:1–5)
                  - Jb Gold, Lebanon, and daughters of Jerusalem (3:6–11)
                  - Jc "Your eyes . . . hair . . . teeth," etc. (4:1–7)
                    - K Myrrh, spice, honey, wine, milk (4:8–15)
                      - L In the garden (4:16)
                      - L' In the garden (5:1a)
                    - K' Myrrh, spice, honey, wine, milk (5:1b)
                  - Ja' "The watchmen found me" (5:2–9)
                  - Jb' Gold, Lebanon and daughters of Jerusalem (5:10–6:1)
                  - Jc' "Your eyes . . . hair . . . teeth," etc. (6:4–12)
                - I' "My beloved is mine" (6:2–3)
              - H' "Vineyards" (6:13–7:12a)
            - G' Fragrance and blossoming (7:12b–13)
          - F' "His left hand" (8:1–5)
        - E' "House" (8:6–7)
      - D' Description of the beloved (8:8–9)
    - C' "My own vineyard" (8:10–12)
  - B' Friends (8:13)
- A' Come away together (8:14)

Purpose

Throughout church history, scholars have debated how to interpret the Song of Solomon. Many have taken the book as being allegorical concerning the church's relationship with Jesus. In this interpretation, the emphasis of the book is on our spiritual union with Christ. The argument is that the book uses an illustration of marital joy to speak about the greatest of all joy, which is our relationship with Christ. While this has been an approach to interpreting the book in church history, it is not the best way to understand the author's intention.

Three times in the book an imperative is given to the effect of "Do not stir up or awaken love until it pleases." This is seen in Song of Solomon 2:7; 3:5; and 8:4. In all three instances the imperative is directed towards the daughters of Jerusalem.

Song of Solomon speaks to the physical and emotional attraction between a man and a woman, but important parameters are put within the book. Early within the book, the marriage takes place between Solomon and his betrothed. In all three instances of this phrase, the beloved warned her friends that they should not try to conjure up or manufacture this love.

The book should be taken at face value. This book is a celebration of the love between a man and a woman. The book uses a great deal of metaphor and imagery to speak of this relationship between the man and the woman. In no way is this book crude or tactless. The book speaks of the maturity, the beauty, and the satisfaction that comes from a God-honoring relationship between a man and a woman.

> **Song of Solomon Purpose Statement:** The relationship between the bride and the bridegroom is celebrated.

Reflection questions:

1. Why should the Song of Solomon be taken as a love song between a husband and a wife and not allegorically as some kind of metaphor for Christ and the church?

2. What is the development of the relationship in Song of Solomon and what does that tell us about how God has structured the relationship between a man and a woman?

3. How is beauty to be understood in Song of Solomon? Is it just a matter of physical characteristics? Is it only in the eyes of the beholder?

6

Isaiah

THE NAME *ISAIAH* IN Hebrew means "Yahweh saves." This is perfectly fitting for this prophet who gave the most description of the future restoration and redemption of Israel.

Isaiah is the second-most-quoted Old Testament book within the New Testament, second only to Psalms. Paul especially made use of Isaiah in his many epistles. Paul's theological argument within Romans hinged on the future restoration of Israel. Within Romans, Paul made the argument that God brings about salvation for His chosen people, a salvation that cannot be undone.

The antagonist within Romans asked the question about Israel: If Israel has been done away with, then how can we trust that God will save us? Didn't God promise to save Israel?

Paul responded by pointing to the Old Testament promises made to Israel. In Romans 11 Paul said that God has not ultimately rejected His people. Instead, God will work with Israel in the future again. The Gentiles had been grafted in to God's promises, but this did not abrogate God's promises to Israel.

In Romans 11:25–26, Paul said, "I do not want you, brethren, to be uninformed of this mystery . . . that a partial hardening has happened to Israel, until the fullness of the Gentiles has come in. And in this way all Israel will be saved."

Immediately after this Paul quoted from Isaiah 59:

> "The Deliverer will come from Zion,
> He will remove ungodliness from Jacob."
> "This is My covenant with them
> When I take away their sins."

Paul's argument was that God can be trusted because He always keeps His promises. If He promises salvation to us, He will save us. If He promised salvation to Israel, then we should fully expect He will do exactly as He said. However, the promises to Israel have not been finalized yet. They were not finalized in Paul's day, nor are they finalized today, more than 2000 years later. But Paul based his foundational theology in the prophecies of Isaiah. Paul argued in Romans 11:15 that if the partial rejection of Israel means that the gospel now comes to the Gentiles, what will Israel's full acceptance mean but life from the dead.

Isaiah spoke of the judgment that was to come upon Israel because of their wickedness, Israel's future restoration, the New Covenant, and most importantly, the coming Anointed One who would save His people.

Isaiah's theology was robust, providing the foundation for much of the theology seen in the New Testament. This pinnacle Old Testament book demands our time and attention if we are to understand the argument and the theology it contains.

Structure

As with the other Major Prophets, the structure of Isaiah has been debated for quite some time. The book has a clear distinction between Isaiah 1–39 and 40–66. The traditional way to see the structure of the book is to realize that chapters 1 through 39 speak oracles of condemnation (with chapters 36 through 39 giving a historical connection) and chapters 40 through 66 speak oracles of comfort to the Jews.

Because there is such a stark contrast between these two major portions of Isaiah, some scholars argue that this book had more than one author. However, we need to understand the structure in light of Isaiah's intention. Just as with other prophets, especially Ezekiel, the contrast between judgment and restoration is emphasized. The first portion of the book spoke clearly to the judgment that was to come upon Israel because of their wickedness. The latter part of the book gave great hope to Israel that they were to be rescued and redeemed.

The contrast is apparent because God, as a God of mercy and kindness, keeps His promises to restore Israel. However, Israel was full of wickedness and rebellion, which God, as a just God, must punish.

An argument is also made that the book of Isaiah is a chiasm. In this argument, chapters 1 through 12 give oracles of judgment and future restoration. This would be mirrored in chapters 58 through 66 at the end of the book.

Moving closer to the center, chapters 13 through 27 speak to the humiliation of the Babylonian king. This would be mirrored in chapters 49 through 57 with the description of the exaltation of the humble servant who is to come. Chapters 28 through 35 state that Israel is not to trust in any earthly power. This would be mirrored in chapters 40 through 48, which emphasize the powerlessness of false gods and idols. This places the center of the chiasm in chapters 36 through 39, which are narratives speaking about God's sovereignty and absolute divine power.

It is clear that at the center of Isaiah are these narratives, but at times scholars can overemphasize chiasms in the Old Testament. An important question to ask in terms of the structure of the book is why the genre switches two narratives in this central portion.

Looking at the book as a chiasm can help to answer this question, but some of the portions that are meant to mirror each other do not fit neatly together. It is best to see the structure of Isaiah in the following way:

Isaiah 1–39	Oracles of condemnation	
	Isaiah 1–35	Israel's coming judgment
	Isaiah 36–37	Hezekiah and Assyria's defeat
	Isaiah 38–39	Hezekiah and the Babylonian threat
Isaiah 40–66	Oracles of comfort	
	Isaiah 40–41	Yahweh is for Israel
	Isaiah 42–44	Yahweh's servant
	Isaiah 45	God's sovereignty over Cyrus
	Isaiah 46–48	Israel and Babylon
	Isaiah 49–59	Salvation through God's servant
	Isaiah 60–66	Israel's future exaltation

Purpose

A central emphasis of the book is the description of God as holy. We will discuss this in more detail in the themes below; this idea is central to the entire purpose of Isaiah.

We must understand the tension between the future judgment of Israel and the future restoration promised to Israel in light of God's character. God is both holy and compassionate. Therefore, He cannot abide with any wickedness in His people. But His loving kindness means that He does not just do away with His people, but instead, brings about their salvation and future perfection.

Isaiah Purpose Statement: Holy Yahweh will perfectly purify His unholy people by sending His servant, the Messiah, for their salvation and restoration.

Themes

The Holy One of Israel

God gave Himself this title 25 times throughout the book of Isaiah. He also called Himself "the Holy One of Jacob" and more simply "the Holy One." As we will discuss in the chapter on Ezekiel, there are a few instances in the Old Testament of God revealing Himself in His holiness. Ezekiel 1 is an example of this. But perhaps the most well-known example of this is Isaiah 6, in which Isaiah has a vision of God on His throne.

Isaiah 6 paints a picture of God sitting on His throne surrounded by angels. The weight of His glory fills the throne room, which is in His temple. The angels that surround Him are called seraphim. This title is from the Hebrew word for burning. But even these burning ones must cover their faces before holy God. They cry out constantly, "Holy, holy, holy is Yahweh of hosts; the whole earth is full of His glory!"

Isaiah, a human, was given this vision, and his immediate response was to fall on his face in recognition of his own unholiness. One of the angels purified Isaiah, and Isaiah was commissioned as a prophet and sent out. Isaiah 6:8 says, "Then I heard the voice of the Lord, saying, 'Whom shall I send, and who will go for Us?' Then I said, 'Here am I. Send me!'"

Isaiah was sent out as God's mouthpiece, speaking against the wickedness of Israel, calling them to repentance.

Israel had treated the holiness of God lightly. To satisfy their own appetites and cravings, they had put the holiness of God out of their minds, acting as though God did not see or care about their wickedness.

God reminded them through Isaiah and the other prophets that He sees and knows all. God reminded them again and again that He is the Holy One of Israel. His holiness will not be treated lightly. His perfection will not be downplayed. Holy God would not abide with the wickedness of His people.

This theme is seen throughout Isaiah but also in the rest of the Bible. Even in the Sermon on the Mount, Jesus gave the command, "Therefore, you are to be perfect, as your heavenly Father is perfect." (Matt. 5:48).

The problem that all mankind has had after the fall, and the problem which is most on display in the example of the nation of Israel, is the issue of how an unholy people can have a relationship with a holy God.

The Anointed One

This brings us to the next central theme in Isaiah, the Messiah. The issue mentioned above is only remedied through the work of the Messiah.

Isaiah is a beacon of gospel truth in the Old Testament. Isaiah 53 is the best-known chapter in Isaiah, if not in all of the Old Testament. This chapter holds the description of the suffering servant, sent from God to be a substitutionary sacrifice for the atonement of His people.

The theological foundation of substitutionary atonement is laid with statements such as Isaiah 53:10, "But the Lord was pleased / To crush Him," and Isaiah 53:7, "Like a lamb that is led to slaughter, / And like a sheep that is silent before its shearers, / So He did not open His mouth," and Isaiah 53:11, "By His knowledge the Righteous One, / My Servant, will justify the many, / As He will bear their iniquities."

God sent His Messiah, the Suffering Servant, to make atonement for His people, to make an unholy people holy so that they could have relationship with a holy God. After the fall of humans into sin, no progress could be made without this substitutionary atonement.

Isaiah also depicts the Messiah as the King and Conqueror. Isaiah 52:15 says, "Kings will shut their mouths on account of Him."

God will be exalted over all His creation. The Messiah will rule from Jerusalem, delivering perfect justice and establishing perfect peace.

God's Comfort

An additional theme that is important to recognize in Isaiah—though there are many themes that can be seen throughout the book—is the idea of God's comfort. God is holy, and He requires His people to be holy. His people are full of wickedness because we are born into sin. But through the Messiah, God creates a way for an unholy people to be holy and to have relationship with Him.

God brings about the salvation of His people, a work that brings God glory. God does not only bring about the salvation of His people, but He also promises perfect comfort for His people. As we saw in Ecclesiastes and Job, in the current world, humanity suffers, and life is full of pain and grief.

Isaiah spoke a great deal about coming judgment, but Isaiah also spoke of God making all things right in the end.

Isaiah 65:17–19 prophesies,

> "For behold, I create new heavens and a new earth;
> and the former things will not be remembered or come to mind.

> "But be glad and rejoice forever in what I create;
> For behold, I create Jerusalem *for* rejoicing
> And her people *for* gladness.
> "I will also rejoice in Jerusalem and be glad in My people;
> And there will no longer be heard in her
> the voice of weeping and the sound of crying.

God promises to provide for every need of His people. Isaiah 55:1 says, "Ho! Every one who thirsts, come to the waters; / And you who have no money, come, buy and eat!"

Isaiah 56 also speaks to the salvation that is to come to the Gentiles. This comfort and blessing is not just for the nation of Israel, but for all who love God.

God promised perfect comfort for His people. The promises of future restoration are not spiritualized or abstract.

Isaiah spoke of the tangible nature of God's blessing and comfort. Isaiah 51:3 says,

> Indeed, the Lord will comfort Zion;
> He will comfort all her waste places.
> And her wilderness He will make like Eden,
> And her desert like the garden of the LORD;
> Joy and gladness will be found in her,
> Thanksgiving and the sound of a melody.

God not only described Himself as the Holy One of Israel, not only the One who will send the Messiah, but God says of Himself, "I, even I, am He who comforts you" (Isa. 51:12).

Reflection questions:

1. How does Isaiah weave together the ideas of God's holiness, the Messiah's atonement, and the future restoration of all who love God?

2. Why is such a clear distinction seen between Isaiah 1–39 and 40–66? How do judgment and restoration fit together in this book?

3. What prophecies are given in Isaiah of the coming Messiah? Look in particular at Isaiah 7, 9, 11, 32, 43–44, 52–53, and 61.

7

Jeremiah

Jeremiah stands as a foundational book among the Prophets. Jeremiah was called the weeping prophet, a theme seen throughout both Jeremiah and Lamentations. Jeremiah was witness to the destruction and devastation that came upon his own people because of their wickedness.

With his own eyes, he saw the destruction of Jerusalem and the Temple. With his own eyes, he saw his people hauled into captivity into Babylon. It seemed at this point in Israel's history as if there was no hope at all. How many different nations had been carried off into captivity to Babylon never to be heard of again? Again and again the Babylonians demonstrated their military might by conquering people groups that no longer exist today.

Israel was hauled off into exile, and the Babylonians brought new people groups into the land of Israel in order to mix up things and prevent rebellion. It appeared there was no hope for Israel.

But Jeremiah acted as an anchor of hope. A pinnacle text is Jeremiah 33:14–21:

> "Behold, days are coming," declares the Lord, "when I will fulfill the good word which I have spoken concerning the house of Israel and the house of Judah. In those days and at that time I will cause a righteous Branch of David to spring forth; and He shall execute justice and righteousness on the earth. In those days Judah will be saved and Jerusalem will dwell in safety; and this is *the name* by which she will be called: the Lord is our righteousness." For thus says the Lord, "David shall never lack a man to sit on the throne of the house of Israel; and the Levitical priests shall never lack a man before Me to offer burnt offerings, to burn grain offerings and to prepare sacrifices continually."
>
> The word of the Lord came to Jeremiah, saying, "Thus says the Lord, 'If you can break My covenant for the day and My covenant for the night, so that day and night will not be at their appointed time, then My covenant may also be broken with David My servant so that he shall not have a son to reign on his throne, and with the Levitical priests, My ministers.'"

God said that just as sure as the sun would come up daily, He would fulfill His promises to Israel. Nothing in this text in Jeremiah points to this being interpreted as some kind of spiritual Israel. Rather, Jeremiah was adamant that God would fulfill His promises to the nation of Israel, the same nation that went into exile in Babylon because of their wickedness.

Daniel, sitting in exile in Babylon, was so sure about Jeremiah's prophecies, that he anticipated the return from the exile because of Jeremiah's statement about Israel being in exile for seventy years. Daniel 9:2 wrote, "In the first year of his reign, I, Daniel, observed in the books the number of the years which was *revealed as* the word of the LORD to Jeremiah the prophet for the completion of the desolations of Jerusalem, *namely,* seventy years."

This comes from Jeremiah 25:11–12:

> "This whole land will be a desolation and a horror, and these nations will serve the king of Babylon seventy years.
>
> "Then it will be when seventy years are completed I will punish the king of Babylon and that nation," declares the LORD, "for their iniquity, and the land of the Chaldeans; and I will make it an everlasting desolation."

Daniel had a copy of the book of Jeremiah while he was in captivity in Babylon. The book of Jeremiah would have been finished by Jeremiah shortly after the destruction of Jerusalem. Daniel took to heart everything that was written in the book, seeing it as prophecy, which should be taken at face value. Daniel went into exile as a young person, and at the end of his life, recognized that the seventy years of exile were almost finished. Indeed, after seventy years, King Cyrus allowed the Jews to return to Jerusalem.

Just as Daniel took the prophecies of Jeremiah at face value, so should we. Many of Jeremiah's statements about Israel have not yet been fulfilled. As we will see in Jeremiah 31 through 33, God said He would bring Israel from the ends of the earth, restoring them in their own land, which He promised to Abraham, Isaac, and Jacob. God's promises to Israel will all be fulfilled in the same way that the prophecy of the seventy years was fulfilled.

STRUCTURE

Some debate exists about the structure of Jeremiah. But it is possible that the book is written as a chiasm. An introduction in the first three verses emphasizes the captivity of Jerusalem. In parallel with this, chapter 52, the final chapter, retells the destruction of Jerusalem and the exile of the people.

As we move closer to the center of the book, we see that the first ten chapters, not including the introduction, are filled with prophecies against Judah, emphasizing the destruction coming from the north. Parallel to this, chapters 46 through 51 give prophecies against the Gentile nations, speaking also about destruction coming from the north.

Chapters 11 through 20 speak about Judah's exile as do chapters 36 through 45. Chapters 21 through 29 speak about the failure of the then-current king of Judah, Zedekiah, as well as the overall failure of previous kings. This is parallel to chapters 34 and 35, which also speak about Zedekiah and the failure of the previous kings.

This leaves the center of the book as chapters 30 through 33, which provide the prophecy and future hope of the new covenant.

Jeremiah 1:1–3	Introduction: Until the fall of Jerusalem
Jeremiah 1:4–10:25	Prophecies against Judah
Jeremiah 11:1–20:18	Judah's exile
Jeremiah 21:1–29:32	Prophecies about the kings of Judah
Jeremiah 30:1–33:26	The new covenant
Jeremiah 34:1–35:19	Prophecies about the kings of Judah
Jeremiah 36:1–45:5	Judah's exile
Jeremiah 46:1–51:64	Prophecies against the nations
Jeremiah 52:1–34	Appendix: The fall of Jerusalem

Purpose

Jeremiah emphasized the contrast between the Mosaic Covenant and the New Covenant. Israel demonstrated unfaithfulness by consistently breaking the Mosaic Covenant. The Mosaic Covenant was established at Mount Sinai when Moses was leading the people, around 1440 BC. Jeremiah wrote right before, during, and after the destruction of Jerusalem in 586 BC.

So, for century after century, the people would break the Mosaic Law; then God would correct them and seek to restore them. This happened again and again in the period of the Judges after Joshua took the people into the land. This happened during the kingships of Saul, David, and Solomon. And this happened again and again after the divided kingdom, when Israel was split into the northern Kingdom of Israel and the southern Kingdom of Judah. Israel never fulfilled the Mosaic Covenant, and this brought about the destruction that came upon Jerusalem.

Jeremiah is in a long line of prophets who warned people of the coming destruction. They did not repent or respond positively to Jeremiah's preaching. Therefore, Jeremiah not only prophesied about the coming destruction of Jerusalem but also witnessed this destruction.

Jeremiah contrasted Israel's lack of fidelity in the Mosaic Covenant to God's institution of the promised New Covenant. In this New Covenant, God will change the heart of the people and cause them to love Him. This will bring about Israel's full restoration.

This contrast between the Mosaic Covenant and the New Covenant is at the heart of Jeremiah. Israel was not able to save themselves. God must intervene and give them the New Covenant and a new heart or they would perish in their sins forever.

> **JEREMIAH PURPOSE STATEMENT:** Jerusalem and the Temple were destroyed because of Israel's lack of faithfulness in the Mosaic Covenant, but God promised the New Covenant by which He will fully restore His people.

THEMES

Persecution

Jeremiah suffered many things at the hands of the Jewish leaders while he prophesied. One of the themes in the book is the persecution he endured. This is set up in the introduction to the book in Jeremiah 1:18–19. God told Jeremiah that he would be a strong tower, a fortified city against the whole land of Judah.

Jeremiah stood against the kings of Judah, its officials, its priests, and the people of the land. Verse 19 says these all would fight against Jeremiah, but would not prevail against him because God was with him. When Jeremiah began his prophetic career, the road forward was one of persecution in trial and distress.

Jeremiah 26 shows a prime example of the suffering Jeremiah endured. Many false priests and false prophets heard what Jeremiah was saying and devised schemes to try to put him to death. Jeremiah 26:14 is a statement Jeremiah made, noting that he was willing to be put to death for the message he was preaching.

Jeremiah 37–38 tells of Jeremiah being imprisoned and beaten as the Babylonians came against Jerusalem. After this, Jeremiah was cast into a cistern and left for dead until he was rescued by a man named Ebed-melech.

Jeremiah was called the weeping prophet not just because he saw the destruction of Jerusalem from a distance. He experienced the destruction of Jerusalem, the starvation, as well as the persecution by the Jewish leaders because of the message he was preaching.

Jeremiah stands as an exemplar of the prophets God sent to Israel and to Judah, who were persecuted for the sake of Yahweh. Hebrews 11 makes the prophets an entire category of faith-filled people. They conquered kingdoms, enforced justice, obtained promises, and accomplished great things for the Lord (Heb. 11:32–33). But they were also described as being tortured, suffering mocking and flogging, suffering imprisonment, and even being stoned and martyred for their message.

Hebrews 11:38 says the world was not worthy of all of these. They refused to accept an easier life so they might be resurrected to a better life. Jeremiah stands as an example of these ones who, by faith, proclaimed the truth of God. They refused to water down their message. They refused to compromise the truth, and they suffered incredibly for it.

It is also interesting to note that Jeremiah's life has many parallels to the life of Jesus. In Jeremiah 9:1, Jeremiah wept over Jerusalem, just as Jesus did in Luke 19:41. In Jeremiah 7, the prophet spoke out against the money changers in the Temple, just as Jesus did in Matthew 21:13.

Both Jeremiah and Jesus were imprisoned and tried by the Jewish leaders. Both foretold the destruction of Jerusalem and of the Temple. In Mark 13, Jesus spoke about the coming destruction of Jerusalem and the Temple, which occurred in AD 70.

Jeremiah's message centered around his prophecy of the coming destruction, which occurred in 586 BC. Both Jesus and Jeremiah suffered at the hands of the people they were trying to minister to. They both were speaking truths, calling the people to repentance.

The example of Jeremiah's life is an encouragement for us today to help us think past our current circumstances and our current suffering, looking to the resurrection and the new world that is to come.

The New Covenant

Several different covenants are mentioned throughout the Old Testament. The first covenant mentioned is the covenant made with Noah in Genesis 9. This is a covenant of time. God simply promised that He would not destroy the world with the flood, no matter how wicked mankind would get. God promised to deal with humans and work with them for a particular period of time that only He knows. God would never again wipe out the world with a flood and seek to start over.

The next covenant established by God was the Abrahamic Covenant. This comes only a few chapters after the Noahic Covenant. God established this covenant with Abraham in Genesis 15. Specifically, God promised to give Abraham a land, descendants, and blessing.

Out of all the groups in the world at that time, God decided to work with Abraham and to work out His plan of redemption through the seed of Abraham. Throughout Genesis, the focus on genealogies continues to narrow down how God will work out His redemption of the world through the seed of Abraham.

The next covenant established was the Mosaic Covenant. We see this in several different locations in the Old Testament because the people continued to break the Mosaic Covenant and new stipulations were given.

After the people left Egypt, they came to Mount Sinai, and God established His covenant with them (Exod. 19). The people quickly agreed that they would abide by everything written in the covenant. However, the people were not able to abide by the covenant because they did not have a heart to love God or follow after God.

The Ten Commandments, which were given within this Mosaic Covenant, were only an external set of laws for the people. Because their hearts were not changed, they constantly broke the laws, thereby needing atonement. Within the Mosaic Covenant, God established parameters for the people to make sacrifices to atone for their sin. But as the people quickly learned, the blood of bulls and goats did not change their wicked hearts.

This covenant was reiterated in Deuteronomy 29 and 30. But even though the covenant was renewed, Moses told the people that they would not abide by the covenant because their hearts had not changed.

Another often-overlooked covenant is the one made with Phinehas in Numbers 25. Phinehas was the son of Eleazar, the son of Aaron the priest. Because Phinehas was zealous to destroy the wickedness among the people of Israel when they were guilty of adultery and idolatry with the Moabites, God promised a covenant of perpetual priesthood for the line of Phinehas, to be priests before God forever.

The next covenant was made with King David in Second Samuel 7. God promised to have a descendant of David as king on David's throne in Jerusalem forever. This is why it was so important for Matthew to trace Jesus' lineage back through David because Jesus is the true King who will rule from David's throne forever.

The culminating covenant was the New Covenant. Moses spoke about the need for a new covenant even as he arbitrated the Mosaic Covenant with the people of Israel. Isaiah, Jeremiah, Ezekiel, and the twelve Minor Prophets also spoke about the New Covenant in Jeremiah 31–33, which gave the most description of the New Covenant.

This New Covenant was in direct contrast with the Mosaic Covenant. The Mosaic Covenant was external, subsisting only in laws written down, which the people were to follow. But external laws do not change the heart. Throughout the Old Testament, we see the need for a new heart. This New Covenant promises a new heart for the people.

Jeremiah 31:33 says, "'But this is the covenant which I will make with the house of Israel after those days,' declares the Lord, 'I will put My law within them and on their heart I will write it; and I will be their God, and they shall be My people."

Israel would never again stray from the Lord. They would truly love the Lord with the heart God would give to them. Just as God promised, they would be His people and He would be their God. God said He would forgive their iniquity, and He would remember their sin no more.

Verse 35 of this chapter establishes the surety of this covenant on the fixed order of the heavens. Only if the sun ceases to shine and the moon and the stars cease to exist, if this fixed order departs, then Israel would cease from being a nation before God.

We can be certain that God will fulfill His promises for His people, Israel, exactly as He promised. These promises are not spiritualized, they are not given away to another people. They are for Israel, and God will fulfill them because of His faithfulness.

Reflection questions:

1. Why do you think the Jewish leaders persecuted Jeremiah so much because of the message he preached?

2. How is the New Covenant different from all covenants that came before it?

3. How can we be certain that God will continue to work with His people and keep His promises to them?

4. If God continues to work with His people, Israel, then how does this give us assurance of God's promises made to us?

8

Lamentations

OUR ENGLISH TITLES FOR the books in the Old Testament are different than the titles used in Hebrew. Traditionally, the Hebrew titles are just the first word of the book. So, for example, we use the English title of the book of Genesis because the book has to do with beginnings. However, in Hebrew the title for this book is the first Hebrew word of the book which is "In the beginning."

Lamentations is the English title used for the book we're looking at now because of its content. Interestingly, the Hebrew title for this short book is the first word of the book, which in Hebrew is the word for "how." The full phrase used to begin the book is the statement, "How lonely sits the city that was full of people!"

This Hebrew title, "How," is fitting when we try to understand what this book describes. We might ask some additional "how" questions. How did it come to this? How has this happened? We might make exclamatory statements as well. How horrible is the destruction that came upon Jerusalem! How awful is the suffering of the people!

Jeremiah wrote Lamentations, which is why this short book follows the book of Jeremiah. Even today, religious Jews annually read this book that commemorates the fall of Jerusalem.

Jeremiah was called the weeping prophet because of all the devastation he witnessed. Lamentations was written right after the fall of Jerusalem in 586 BC. The Babylonians invaded Judah several times, but 586 marks the full, final invasion leading to the complete destruction of Jerusalem. The Temple was destroyed, the walls were broken down, the people were led away into exile. The Babylonians did not let conquered people remain in their own land. They did this so there would be less incentive to rebel. Indeed, some Jews were left but they were poor and insignificant politically.

Jeremiah warned of this coming destruction in the book of Jeremiah, and after it came to pass, he spoke about its devastation in this short book of Lamentations.

Structure

The structure of Lamentations is intricate. This book has five chapters that can easily be divided into five sections. Each chapter is a lament. Chapter 1 laments the devastation of Jerusalem. Chapter 2 emphasizes the Lord's punishment of Judah's sin. Chapter 3 is a lengthy response of Jeremiah to this punishment and devastation. Chapter 4 also begins with the word "how," and emphasizes the wrath God poured out against Judah.

Chapter 5 begins with a request for God to remember what happened to Judah, to remember His people. The last four verses of the book summarize what came before. Verse 19 reiterates that God reigns forever and is sovereign. Verse 20 is a question directed to God, "Why do you forget us forever?" Verse 21 is a prayer, requesting God to restore Israel. And verse 22 is the cliffhanger, "Unless you have utterly rejected us, and you remain exceedingly angry with us."

The devastation and destruction of Judah and Jerusalem was now part of their history. The question is whether they would be restored in the future or if they would be doomed to disappear in history.

In addition to the chapter breaks and structure of Lamentations, the structure of each chapter is intricate. Similar to Psalm 119, each chapter of Lamentations is alliterated in a particular way. Twenty-two verses comprise chapter 1, each verse beginning with a successive letter of the alphabet.

Chapter 2 starts over with the first letter of the alphabet, *aleph,* and does the same thing that chapter 1 did with 22 verses comprising chapter 2. Chapter 3 has 66 verses and still follows the alliteration pattern, but in triplet. So, verses 1, 2, and 3 all begin with *aleph.* Verses 4, 5, and 6 all begin with the next letter of the Hebrew alphabet, *bet* (the English word "alphabet" is just the first and second letters of the Hebrew alphabet, *aleph* and *bet*).

Chapter 4 goes back to 22 verses, each beginning with a successive letter of the alphabet. Finally, chapter 5 also has 22 verses, but it breaks out of this alliteration pattern.

It's interesting to note the literary devices and poetry Jeremiah used for his lament. Intricacy in poetry is certainly not relegated only to uplifting themes.

Purpose

The most well-known verses of Lamentations are found in chapter 3. The beloved, old hymn, "Great is Thy Faithfulness," comes from these verses. Lamentations 3:22–23 state, "The LORD's lovingkindnesses indeed never cease, / For His compassions never fail. / *They* are new every morning; / Great is Your faithfulness."

This is a beautiful description of God's character, and we should not take it out of its context. Just a few verses before, Jeremiah said that he had forgotten what happiness is. He begged the Lord to remember his affliction, and he said his soul continually remembered his affliction.

The turning point is verse 21 where Jeremiah said, "This I recall to my mind, / Therefore I have hope." He then gave verses 22 and 23, reminding himself of God's faithfulness.

The purpose of the book is certainly to lament the horrid destruction that came upon Jerusalem and Judah. The historical account of this destruction is horrendous. The way Babylon took captives and even wiped out nations was infamous. The Babylonians held nothing back in their quest to squelch any rebellion.

Jeremiah pointed to God's sovereignty in Lamentations 3:37, "Who is there who speaks and it comes to pass, / Unless the Lord has commanded *it*?"

While the Babylonians invaded and destroyed Jerusalem, God used them as an instrument against Judah. Jeremiah understood that none of this happened outside of the Lord's control.

The great tension in the text of Lamentations is how God can demonstrate His wrath against Judah and yet still show compassion and be faithful to His people. Even though God judged the sin and rebellion of His people, they would will not be annihilated. Jeremiah relied on the character of God and the promises of God to hope in the future restoration of Israel.

> **Lamentations Purpose Statement:** Even though God brought judgment on Judah because of their sins, God is faithful and compassionate to bring about their future restoration.

Reflection questions:

1. How is it that God can use a wicked people to bring punishment against His own chosen people?

2. What is the context of Lamentations 3:22–23? How does this context give further weight to Jeremiah's statement in these verses?

3. Do you see any parallels between Lamentations and Job? In what ways are they similar and dissimilar?

9

Ezekiel

SOME DEBATE EXISTS as to when Ezekiel was born, but we think it was around 620 BC. The destruction of Jerusalem by the Babylonians occurred in 586 BC. The Assyrians destroyed the northern kingdom in 722 BC, just to give a time frame.

Jeremiah was called the weeping prophet, and Jeremiah even wrote the short book of Lamentations. But Ezekiel is also full of lamentation. It is one of the Major Prophets, along with Jeremiah and Isaiah. Its 48 chapters contain many visions and things that are difficult to comprehend.

It also includes many examples from Ezekiel's life. For example, in Ezekiel 24, Ezekiel's wife died. Verse 15 says she was the delight of Ezekiel's eyes. He loved her very much, but God took her away from him. Ezekiel's life was a picture of mourning, suffering, and heartache. His life was an example of God's sorrow over Israel's sin.

Ezekiel rose to the heights of revelation as well. Ezekiel 1 is a rare instance in the Old Testament showing the glory of the Lord being revealed. Isaiah 6 is another one of these instances.

Isaiah was given a vision in this chapter of the glory of the Lord, and he responded in absolute humility and repentance. In the first chapter of Ezekiel, Ezekiel was given a vision of the glory of the Lord. Chapter 2 followed this with the call of Ezekiel to be a prophet. From this point on, Ezekiel's job was to call the people to repentance and to foretell the coming destruction because of the wickedness of the Jews.

From the beginning of Ezekiel's ministry, he prophesied that Jerusalem would be destroyed. Ezekiel knew what was coming upon the Jews and Jerusalem, and he knew he could not stop it. But he still called the people to repent, giving them signs, metaphors, and pictures of the coming destruction.

Structure

Ezekiel brings the reader down to the pit of despair with the imagery of the destruction coming upon the Jews. Ezekiel spoke of horrible things that would be done against the Jews because of their rebellion against God. The Temple would be destroyed. Jerusalem would be destroyed. The Jews would suffer at the hands of pagan nations. They would be taken into captivity.

Ezekiel presented the picture of women weeping, crying out because of their dead loved ones. However, the structure of Ezekiel also gave hope. Just as it gave metaphors and pictures of Israel's coming destruction, Ezekiel also painted a picture of a better day that would come.

Ezekiel 40–48 is an interesting portion of the Old Testament, speaking about a future temple within a new Jerusalem. The description given within these chapters has not yet been seen in Israel's history. The temple that is described has never existed in Israel's history. Ezekiel even gave the measurements of the temple. Ezekiel highlights the glory of the Lord within this temple and within this new Jerusalem.

This is contrasted with the glory of the Lord leaving the current Temple in Ezekiel's time, as seen in Ezekiel 10. Ezekiel 10 and 11 are at the heart of the first major portion of the book. Chapters 1–23 speak of the rebellion of the Jews, with the glory of the Lord departing from Israel in Ezekiel 11:23.

Starting in chapter 4 and lasting all the way through Ezekiel 34:10, Ezekiel spoke about the judgment coming from the nations. Ezekiel 24 gives us an important picture of this in the beginning of the siege of Jerusalem. But in this section, Ezekiel also spoke prophecies against other nations, including the Philistia, Tyre, and Egypt.

Chapter 34 through the end of the book discusses the restoration of Israel. The glory of the Lord would return to Israel, but not in the current Temple. God would fight for His people and establish a new order and a new kingdom, with Jerusalem as its capital.

Ezekiel 1:1–3	Introduction of Ezekiel
Ezekiel 1:4–23:49	The rebellion of the Jews
Ezekiel 24:1–34:10	Judgment upon Israel and the nations
Ezekiel 34:11–48:35	The restoration of the Israel
Ezekiel 34:11–34:31	God's covenant of peace
Ezekiel 35	Prophecy against Mt. Seir
Ezekiel 36	Prophecy of the mountains of Israel
Ezekiel 37	The valley of dry bones
Ezekiel 38–39	Prophecy against Gog
Ezekiel 40–48	The new temple

Purpose

Ezekiel shows an intense contrast. The wickedness of the people is contrasted with the holiness of God. The destruction of Jerusalem is contrasted with the new Jerusalem, which is to come and will never see war. The glory of the Lord departs from the Temple of Ezekiel's time. And the glory of the Lord will shine forth from a future temple about which Ezekiel prophesies.

The Jews who were defined by their wickedness and rebellion against God, would be seen in the future as those who loved the Lord wholeheartedly and were perfectly committed to God. This intense contrast points to the purpose of the book. The light shines brightly in the darkness.

> **Ezekiel Purpose Statement:** The destruction of Jerusalem and the Temple is contrasted with the future new Jerusalem and new temple, which demonstrate God's love for His people and fidelity to His promises.

Themes

Knowing God

As with all books in the Old Testament, many themes could be brought out. We have already discussed some of the themes in Ezekiel in Isaiah and Jeremiah. This does not mean there is unnecessary repetition in these three books. Each book has its own purpose and its own emphasis.

Ezekiel clearly speaks about the restoration of Israel, pointing to the New Covenant and the new heart God would give to His people. This promise of the New Covenant was also emphasized in Jeremiah and Isaiah. But one theme that was important to Ezekiel was the idea that Israel will truly know Yahweh. In this book, Ezekiel makes a statement 73 times: "They will know that I am Yahweh."

God is sovereign over all and works in all things, but humanity often views the events of this life as coincidental. Many even appeal to the false idea of karma. The sovereign God and karma are not theologically compatible. Either God is sovereign and rules over all, or you find some other way to explain what goes on within the world, either by means of karma, luck, or even just purposelessness. When something happens in a person's life, he or she is meant to ask, "Why would a sovereign God bring this into my life?"

We see this good question asked in the book of Job. We can also ask this when good things come into our lives. The Lord gives and the Lord takes away, blessed be the name of the Lord, as Job says.

One of Israel's sins was that they did not attribute anything that was going on to them to the work of God. To make allowances for their own sin, they pretended as though God did not see or did not care about anything that they did. When repercussions came upon them they explained them away, not as God correcting them or judging them, but as something that they needed to overcome.

To overcome the Babylonians, Israel trusted in Egypt. For the Jews to make allowances for their wicked lifestyles, they put their trust in false spiritual leaders who told them lies.

A main theme of Ezekiel's prophecy was that God would bring something upon Israel that would force them to recognize God's sovereign hand working. In many instances in Ezekiel, God's judgment was pronounced against Israel, specifying that it would be such a judgment that Israel would understand that Yahweh is God and is sovereign. Ezekiel 5:13 is an example of this, "Thus My anger will be spent and I will satisfy My wrath on them, and I will be appeased; then they will know that I, the Lord, have spoken in My zeal when I have spent My wrath upon them."

God promised to unleash His fury against the wickedness of Israel in such a way that the people would be recognize His hand in judging them.

God also said that Israel would come to recognize Him as sovereign not only because of His judgment against them but also because of Israel's restoration. This is the blessing and the promise God gave to Israel. He would give them a new heart. He would make the New Covenant with them. His glory would come back to dwell with them. There would be a new Jerusalem and a new temple.

God would give Israel a heart to love Him, and they would know that Yahweh is God when He restored them. An example of this is Ezekiel 20:38, "I will purge from you the rebels and those who transgress against Me; I will bring them out of the land where they sojourn, but they will not enter the land of Israel. Thus you will know that I am the Lord."

One final way God would demonstrate His sovereignty would be by His interactions with the Gentile nations. Ezekiel prophesied judgment against several Gentile nations, including Egypt and many smaller nations that surrounded Israel. Both Israel and the Gentile nations would know that Yahweh was God. Ezekiel 36:23 says, "'I will vindicate the holiness of My great name which has been profaned among the nations, which you have profaned in their midst. Then the nations will know that I am the Lord,' declares the Lord God, 'when I prove Myself holy among you in their sight.'"

No one would again be able to discount God's sovereignty. Every knee would bow, and every tongue would confess. The blessing given to Israel was God's promise that He would not do away with them, but would give them a new heart, cause them to love Him, and restore them as His people.

The Temple

The Temple is a central theme in Ezekiel. The Temple in Ezekiel's time had been profaned by the wickedness of Israel. We should remember that the glory of the Lord filled the Temple after Solomon completed and dedicated it. Before this, the glory of the Lord filled the Tabernacle, which was with Israel in their wanderings in the wilderness after Mount Sinai.

From the point of King Solomon until right before the destruction of Jerusalem, the glory of the Lord could be seen in Solomon's temple. The description given of this glory was not only spiritual but was visible.

The people could not enter the most holy place of glory in the Temple, other than the high priest at a very specific time. If anyone entered this holy place, God himself killed them. We can remember the story of Uzzah who touched the ark of the covenant and was struck dead for doing so. Uzzah did not treat the glory of the Lord with the proper honor and respect.

Even while the glory of the Lord was in Solomon's temple, the people became more corrupt throughout their generations. King David died in 971 BC. Solomon, his son, reigned right after that, building the Temple over several years. Jerusalem was destroyed in 586 BC. So, for a period of almost 400 years the glory of the Lord was in Solomon's temple, even while the people were becoming more wicked. The climactic scene within Ezekiel was the glory of the Lord departing from the Temple before the Babylonians destroyed it.

We should also note that when the Jews were allowed to return to Jerusalem and rebuild the Temple, this second temple did not have the glory of the Lord in it in the same way as Solomon's temple did. This second temple, which was enlarged and made even more beautiful by King Herod right before Jesus was born, was a magnificent structure, but it was only a structure.

The Temple is a meeting place between God and those who follow Him. The Temple played an essential part in the life of any God-fearing person in the Old Testament. Even Jesus spent considerable time in the Temple.

Ezekiel prophesied of another temple that will have the glory of the Lord in it. Much debate surrounds the description of this temple. Is it just a spiritual metaphor, or should it be understood as a literal temple?

Ezekiel gives a great deal of specific description for this temple. God even told Ezekiel to go measure the temple. However, the measurements of the temple were like no temple that had been built previously. Therefore, some scholars who do not hold to a future, literal temple understand this temple as being figurative or symbolic. Some will argue that the exiles who returned to Jerusalem should have built this temple, but did not do so.

However, it is best to understand this temple at face value. It was a vision given to Ezekiel of a future, literal temple. In this literal temple, the glory of the Lord will be witnessed.

Ezekiel 43 speaks about this glory of the Lord filling the Temple. Ezekiel 47 says a river will flow out from the Temple.

This description of a river coming from the Temple is a parallel account to Revelation 22, which speaks of the river of life. We should understand this temple as a prophecy that has not yet come to pass.

Just as the Jews should have taken Ezekiel's prophecy of the destruction of Jerusalem at face value, we should take the prophecies that are yet to be fulfilled at face value.

Reflection questions:

1. What are some of the parallels we can see between the book of Ezekiel and the book of Revelation?
2. Why do you think Ezekiel sought to paint such a stark contrast throughout the entire book?
3. How was Ezekiel's life used as a symbol of what God was trying to teach Israel? Do you think it was fair for God to ask this of Ezekiel?

10

Daniel

DANIEL INCLUDES SOME of the best-known Bible stories. It is also one of the most difficult books to interpret because of its prophecy. There are a few characters in the Old Testament about whom nothing bad was said. Moses was a murderer. David was an adulterer. Jacob was deceptive. The list goes on. Even the prophet Elijah grumbled against God from time to time.

But the Bible says nothing negative about Daniel. Ezekiel 14:20 lists Daniel, along with Noah and Job, as exemplars of righteousness. Ezekiel was a contemporary of Daniel. So, the fact that Ezekiel pointed to the righteousness of Daniel demonstrates how well-known Daniel was for his piety and devotion. This is not to say that Daniel did not sin. Daniel, like any other man, was born into sin and desperately needed a savior. However, Daniel, along with a few other people in the Bible, are only spoken of positively.

Part of the reason why the Bible describes Daniel in such a lofty way is to show that God was preserving His people even during their exile. The books of Jeremiah, Ezekiel, and Isaiah displayed the wickedness of Israel. Israel went into exile described as wicked and rebellious people. However, while they were in exile several stories told show God's workings with Israel while they were in exile.

The book of Esther demonstrated God's faithfulness to Israel while in exile. God continued to send prophets to Israel during their exile and after. There is the amazing story of the return from the exile. And Daniel is a shining example of a righteous Jew who determined to be faithful to God even though he was exiled to Babylon.

It would have been easy for Daniel to forget where he was from and indulge in all that Babylon offered. This was the case for many ethnicities and nations that Babylon took into exile. When the Babylonians conquered a nation, they often displaced the people so they would forget where they were from and would be less likely to rebel. This strategy worked for the Babylonians. But Daniel chose to remain faithful to God.

The Babylonians subdued the Jews on several different occasions, leading to a few different deportations to Babylon. The final exile was in 586 BC when all the Jews were exiled except for the poorest and the least significant.

We do not exactly know Daniel's heritage, but he was one of the first to be exiled during the first major conquest by the Babylonians in 605 BC. Daniel went to Babylon as a young man, and even though he rose to power with the Babylonians and later with the Persians, we see no indication that he returned from the exile.

Daniel also would have been in Babylon for 20 years before he witnessed most of the Jews being exiled. The last timestamp we get in the book of Daniel is Daniel 10:1, which specifies that it was the third year of the reign of Cyrus, king of Persia. This would have been 536 BC.

Not only was Daniel depicted as a righteous person who refused to compromise himself, even in exile, Daniel was also given great ability by God in the area of wisdom and interpretation.

Daniel was listed with his three friends, whose Hebrew names were Hananiah, Mishael, and Azariah—better known today as Shadrach, Meshach, and Abed-nego. It is curious that we know these three friends better by their Babylonian names than their Hebrew names.

The name "Daniel" means "God judges." Hananiah means "Yahweh is compassionate." Mishael means "Who is Like God?" And Azariah means "Yahweh helps." The Babylonian names they were given were pagan. For example, Abed-nego means "slave of Nego," a false god of the Babylonians. Daniel himself received a Babylonian name, Belteshazzar.

According to Daniel 1, these four men were given ability in wisdom and skill far beyond their contemporaries. Daniel was given the ability to interpret visions and dreams. This paves the way for much of the rest of the book. A good deal of the book includes narratives, stories that are familiar to many Christians. However, many of the other portions of the book are prophecies, including visions Daniel had.

STRUCTURE

The fact that Daniel includes both narratives and prophecy makes its structure a little difficult to understand. The book was also written in two different languages. Most of the Old Testament was written in Hebrew. However, a few small sections in the Old Testament were in Aramaic.

Daniel 2–7 was written in Aramaic, while the beginning of the book and the last portion were written in Hebrew. This helps us break down the structure and shows the purpose of the book. Daniel 1 introduced Daniel and his friends, the conquest of the Babylonian king, Nebuchadnezzar, and the emphasis on Daniel's faithfulness by his refusal to defile himself by eating the king's food.

Daniel 2 begins the Aramaic section. Chapters 2 through 7 focus on the Gentile nations and God's sovereignty over the Gentile nations. Chapter 2 includes Nebuchadnezzar's dream which Daniel interpreted, showing world history in light of five kingdoms, the first of which was Babylon.

Chapter 3 tells the story of Nebuchadnezzar setting up a statue of himself, requiring all of his subjects to bow down to the statue. Daniel's three friends were on display when they refused to bow to the statue and were thrown into the fiery furnace.

Chapter 4 tells how God delivered them from the fiery furnace and humbled Nebuchadnezzar. Daniel 5 transitions to a later period, when Belshazzar reigned. This is the story of the handwriting on the wall, which was a prophecy that Belshazzar's kingdom would be overtaken, a prophecy fulfilled that very night when the Persians usurped the Babylonians.

Daniel 6 speaks of a Persian king named Darius who threw Daniel into the lion's den. Just like what happened with his three friends in the fiery furnace, Daniel was delivered from the lion's den.

Chapter 7 is a vision given to Daniel concerning five kingdoms. These were the same kingdoms talked about in chapter 2. Chapter 2 and 7 serve as bookends to this Aramaic section within the book.

Daniel 8 included another vision given to Daniel, emphasizing an individual described as the "little horn." Daniel 8:26 says that this vision refers to a far away time in the future.

The little horn is described as someone who will have great power. He will cause great destruction and even try to revolt against God but will ultimately be broken. Daniel 9 gives the story of Daniel praying and God sending an answer to Daniel's prayer by the hand of Gabriel, the angel. Gabriel spoke of seventy weeks during which the Anointed One will be cut off.

Daniel 10–12 speaks of revelation given to Daniel of the time of the end. This will be the final deliverance for Israel, which is described as being "A time of distress such as never occurred since there was a nation until that time" (Dan. 12:1).

These chapters describe a king of the north and a king of the south who war against each other. Ultimately God is seen as the One who controls the rise and fall of nations and the ultimate deliverance for Israel.

Daniel 1 — Daniel and his friends' faithfulness in Babylon

Daniel 2–7 — God's sovereignty over the gentile nations
- Daniel 2 — Five kingdoms
- Daniel 3 — The statue of Nebuchadnezzar
- Daniel 4 — The humbling of Nebuchadnezzar
- Daniel 5 — The humbling of Belshazzar
- Daniel 6 — Daniel in the lions' den
- Daniel 7 — Daniel's vision of five kingdoms

Daniel 8–12 — God's protection and exaltation of Israel
- Daniel 8 — The little horn
- Daniel 9 — The seventy weeks
- Daniel 10–12 — The ultimate deliverance of Israel

PURPOSE

Even though the book of Daniel includes both narrative and prophecy, the purpose of the book can be seen in all these elements. The emphasis of the book is God's sovereignty, especially considering the gentile nations, the history of the world, and the deliverance and exaltation of Israel.

God is the one who controls human history for His own purposes. Humans have such short lifespans and cannot understand the full scope and movement of history over the course of millennia. However, God controls the rise and fall of nations for His own purposes and for His own glory.

God's selection of Israel, and His continuing work with Israel, is seen both in the individual life of Daniel and in the rise and fall of world empires. Human pride is nothing in comparison with the power of God.

This is seen in prophecy, which can only come about because of the sovereign working and providence of God. It is also seen in fascinating stories such as the humbling of Nebuchadnezzar, the most powerful man in the world in his time.

DANIEL PURPOSE STATEMENT: God's sovereignty over the events of human history demonstrates His glory and providence.

Themes

The Sovereignty of God in Prophecy

A good deal of controversy surrounds the book of Daniel and the prophecies in it. Both scholars and churchgoers debate the nature of the prophecies that are given, the timeline of events, and the specificities that we see within the text.

It is important to note that Daniel was writing down the visions that he saw, giving the best description he could. However, even Daniel had difficulty understanding some of the visions that were given to him.

This is an encouragement to us, who find ourselves thousands of years removed from Daniel. It is a normal pattern within the book of Daniel to see a vision given and then to read the interpretation given after that. For example, Daniel 8 reveals the vision of the ram and the goat. Starting in verse 15, Daniel, who was perplexed about the vision, was given an interpretation of the vision.

The angel Gabriel explained to Daniel some of the details and interpretation of the vision. Gabriel explained that the ram represented the Persian Empire. The goat was the king of Greece. In the vision, the goat had a large horn, which was broken off with four other, smaller horns rising in its place. This represents Alexander the Great and the four kingdoms that his empire was divided into after his death.

Some of the specificity of the prophecies that are given, such as this prophecy about Alexander the Great, leads some scholars to argue that the book of Daniel could only have been written after the events that are described. However, this is not the best way to view the book of Daniel.

Many debates surround the dating of the book. But the prophecies given in the book point to the sovereignty of God, who chose to reveal portions of His plans to those who trust Him. God is sovereign and at times revealed His purposes and plans to individuals in history.

One of the key themes of the book is how the sovereignty of God is on display in the given prophecies. God has no need to reveal His plans to humanity. Daniel is one of those points in the Bible when God demonstrated His control by revealing the future. If God were not sovereign, there would be no absolute certainty of any prophecy.

We can see that several of the prophecies given to Daniel came to fruition within human history. Some of the prophecies that were given have not yet occurred.

Just as with the prophecies of the coming Messiah, the prophecies that we see in Daniel, whether already fulfilled or not yet fulfilled, show us a God who is involved with His creation and is sovereign over it.

Timeline of World History

Humans are fascinated and even obsessed with having an enduring legacy. There is a desire within humans to be remembered past their own lifetimes. But when you think about the scope of history and all the wars and events and accomplishments and failures, most humans are forgotten—at least by other humans. God knows all.

The irony is that the unsaved person tries to forget God all of his or her life, seeking instead to create a legacy that will endure past himself or herself. However, in the end, the human is forgotten by all except God. Ecclesiastes 3 speaks of this. Solomon, in Ecclesiastes, explained that God has orchestrated things this way, the endless cycles of life and death in the world, in order that humans would remember that God is sovereign, and they are not.

Nebuchadnezzar is a prime example of this in Daniel. I would challenge you to try to remember any other king of the Babylonian Empire. What about any king of the Assyrian Empire? The Persian Empire?

Most of us will remember Alexander the Great from the Greek Empire, but unless someone is a scholar of Greek history, no other names of Greek kings will come to mind. Each of the kings of each one of these empires believed they were establishing a dynasty and a legacy that would cause their name to endure. But God is the one who exalts and the one who humbles.

Daniel 4 tells the story of King Nebuchadnezzar, who was the supreme ruler over the Babylonian Empire until his death. Interestingly, chapter 4 is partially told from Nebuchadnezzar's perspective. He said he was walking on the roof of his royal palace in Babylon, and he said to himself, "Is this not Babylon the great, which I myself have built as a royal residence by the might of my power and for the glory of my majesty?" (Dan. 4:30).

But while the words were still in his mouth, God struck him with madness. Nebuchadnezzar went from being the most powerful ruler in the world at the time to being driven away from society, eating grass like an ox, and letting his hair grow long until he looked like a madman.

In verse 34 Nebuchadnezzar says that at the end of these days he looked to heaven, acknowledging that God is sovereign, and Nebuchadnezzar was restored. Nebuchadnezzar's words are:

For His dominion is an everlasting dominion,
And His kingdom *endures* from generation to generation.
All the inhabitants of the earth are accounted as nothing.
But He does according to His will in the host of heaven
And *among* the inhabitants of earth;
And no one can ward off His hand
Or say to Him, "What have you done?"

(Dan. 4:34–35)

Sadly, one of the successors to Nebuchadnezzar, Belshazzar, did not take these words to heart. Belshazzar was humbled in his pride, leading to his own downfall and death. This account in Daniel 5 is another example of God's sovereignty over empires as well as individuals. The timeline of world history is not determined solely based on human ingenuity or human accomplishments. The timeline of world history is controlled by God.

Daniel is important for any study of prophecy because it gives details of this timeline. The timeline is told in terms of four empires. The first empire is the Babylonian Empire, which arose out of the Assyrian Empire.

The second is the Persian Empire, which overtook the Babylonian Empire in the reign of Belshazzar. The third empire is the Greek Empire, with specific description given of Alexander the Great and the division of the empire after Alexander.

The fourth empire is the Roman Empire. Daniel 7 describes the fourth kingdom. Verse 23 says, "The fourth beast will be a fourth kingdom on earth, which will be different from all the *other* kingdoms and will devour the whole earth and tread it down and crush it."

Verse 24 continues to say that out of this empire ten kings shall arise and then another king after them. This king who arises after the ten kings with their kingdoms will be the last king before the Messiah rules. This king described in Daniel should be equated with the Antichrist described in Revelation.

It is important to note that much debate exists about the details of the prophecies in Daniel. Many books have been written dealing with the nuances, and many different interpretations have been given.

It is important to take the prophecies at face value whenever possible. But even doing so does not always yield a perfectly clear picture of what is to come. One difficulty is the interpretation of the seventy weeks in Daniel 9.

Daniel was told that seventy weeks were decreed concerning the Jews and the holy city. At the end of those seventy weeks, everlasting righteousness would be brought in, referring to the rule of the Messiah. The weeks were divided into sixty-two weeks, seven weeks, and one final week.

The timeline began with the command by Cyrus for the exiles to return to Jerusalem and rebuild the city. The sixty-two weeks and seven weeks would be a troubled time after which the Anointed One would be cut off. The final week is described as being a time of war and abomination. At the end of the final week, judgment would be poured out against the Antichrist.

There is debate as to what has already been fulfilled in Daniel's prophecies and what is yet to come. It is key to note that Daniel referred to an individual who is called a desolator, a king, and even an antagonist.

Revelation picked up on this idea in its description of the Antichrist. The Messiah will overthrow this Antichrist, bringing in His own kingdom, which will endure forever.

Reflection questions:

1. What is the relationship between the well-known stories that are told and the prophecies that are in Daniel? Why is the book structured the way that it is, with both narratives and prophecy?

2. Why do you think some prophecies are given interpretations, and some are not?

3. Angels play an important role in the book of Daniel. Why do you think they keep coming up again and again in the book?

4. What are the different descriptions that Daniel gives of the coming Antichrist? How does this contrast with the descriptions given of the coming Messiah and His kingdom?

11

HOSEA

THE TWELVE MINOR Prophets should be thought of as a unified collection. In general, these twelve Minor Prophets are ordered chronologically. The introduction to the book of Hosea places the time of Hosea's ministry in the days of Uzziah, Jotham, Ahaz, and Hezekiah, kings of Judah; and in the days of Jeroboam, the son of Joash, king of Israel.

The Jeroboam referenced here is Jeroboam II, who would have ruled over the northern kingdom of Israel from the early to the mid eighth century BC. He has the same name as Jeroboam, who was the first king of the northern kingdom of Israel in the tenth century BC.

No king of northern Israel is depicted as being godly, and Hosea is one of the key prophets who speaks against the northern kingdom of Israel. Hosea's name in Hebrew means "salvation," and this book, while speaking judgment against the wickedness of Israel, also proclaims God's promise of salvation and restoration to Israel.

The book of Hosea is one of the more well-known of the twelve because of the command God gave to Hosea to marry an adulteress named Gomer. This command that God gave Hosea was meant to be a picture of the adultery of northern Israel, especially during the reign of Jeroboam II in the eighth century BC

Israel had turned away from God and broken the covenant with God. So, God sent His prophets against the northern kingdom to speak out against their wickedness and to turn them back to God.

Of the twelve Minor Prophets, Hosea, Amos, and Jonah focus specifically on the northern kingdom of Israel before the capture of Israel by Assyria in 722 BC.

STRUCTURE

The structure of the book of Hosea can be seen as a series of judgments and restorations. This is all painted with the picture of Hosea's marriage to

Gomer at the beginning of the book. In chapter 1, God commanded Hosea to marry a woman who was not faithful.

Gomer gave birth to three children with Hosea, and they were given names as an indictment against Israel. The name of the firstborn son was Jezreel. God said He would break Israel in the valley of Jezreel. The second child was a daughter named Lo-ruhamah, which means in Hebrew, "No Mercy." God said that He would show no mercy to Israel. The third child was a son named Lo-ammi, which means in Hebrew, "Not My People."

However, chapter 1 ends with a statement of restoration for Israel. Verse 10 says, "And in the place / Where it was said to them, / 'You are not My people,' / It will be said to them, / '*You are* the sons of the living God.'"

Chapter 1 gives a foundational example of judgment declared against Israel and followed by a promise of restoration. Chapter 2 follows this same pattern with the unfaithfulness of Israel put on display. But also, starting in verse 14, God spoke of the future restoration of Israel when He will speak tenderly to her and Israel will call God, "My Husband." Chapter 3 is a short narrative section that speaks to Hosea redeeming his wife. Gomer left Hosea for a life of adultery. But Hosea brought her back as his wife, this story being an example of the faithfulness of God toward Israel.

Chapters 4 through 14 are a cycle of indictments against Israel followed by promises of restoration. This first cycle is from Hosea 4:4 to Hosea 6:3. In this cycle God indicted Israel for having no true knowledge of Him. A key verse is Hosea 4:6, in which God said, "My people are destroyed for lack of knowledge."

Hosea 5:15–6:3 is a picture of Israel turning back to God, which includes the statement, "Let us press on to know the Lord" (Hos. 6:3).

Hosea 6:4–11:11 is an indictment against Israel for having no loyalty toward God. In contrast to God's covenant faithfulness and loyalty, Israel was quick to turn away. God warned in chapter 8 that Israel would reap the whirlwind. However, in Hosea 11:8–11, God gave hope of restoration. God said that His compassion grows warm and tender toward Israel, a sign of His continued covenant faithfulness to them. Hosea 11:12–14:8 reveals the third indictment against Israel, which includes a promise of restoration at the start of chapter 14. This indictment against Israel began with the statement that Israel surrounded God with lies.

Not only did Israel not have true knowledge of God and not only did they not have any loyalty toward God, but they did not have the truth. They justified their wickedness by perverting the truth.

Even after all of this, there is still hope of restoration. God promised that He would heal Israel, and Israel would return to Him and be established. The last verse of Hosea is a call for wisdom, a plea for Israel to understand these things. The structure of Hosea can be outlined:

Hosea 1:1	Introduction
Hosea 1:2–9	The marriage of Hosea and Gomer
Hosea 1:10–2:1	God's promise of restoration
Hosea 2:2–13	Israel's adultery
Hosea 2:14–23	God's promise of restoration
Hosea 3:1–3	The restoration of Hosea and Gomer
Hosea 3:4–5	God's promise of restoration
Hosea 4:1–6:3	The first indictment
Hosea 4:1–19	Israel's lack of knowledge
Hosea 5:1–14	Judgment pronounced
Hosea 5:15–6:3	God's promise of restoration
Hosea 6:4–11:11	The second indictment
Hosea 6:4–7:16	Israel's lack of loyalty
Hosea 8:1–11:7	Judgment pronounced
Hosea 11:8–11	God's promised restoration
Hosea 11:12–14:8	The third indictment
Hosea 11:12–13:3	Israel's lack of truth
Hosea 13:4–16	Judgment pronounced
Hosea 14:1–8	God's promised restoration
Hosea 14:9	The call to understand

PURPOSE

The purpose of the Hosea is a clear contrast between Israel and God. God always demonstrated His faithfulness even though Israel broke the covenant and rebelled against Him. God was faithful to Israel, and He also promised to bring restoration, which would lead Israel to return to Him.

HOSEA PURPOSE STATEMENT: Even though Israel is unfaithful, God's faithfulness will bring about the restoration of Israel.

Themes

Of course, the central theme of Hosea is faithfulness. But we can also see a few other themes throughout the book. This includes the war between truth and lies and the true knowledge of God.

Knowledge of God/Truth and Lies

In Hosea 4:1, God indicted Israel for having no knowledge of Him. We should understand that this is not as though Israel had no understanding of God at all. Rather, Israel had twisted their understanding of God to accommodate their wickedness. They justified their sin by perverting their true understanding of God's character.

God said that no one in Israel truly understood His character. This is a theme that we will see in many of the Minor Prophets. The prophecy of Hosea came at a point in Israel's history when wickedness was rampant. When we look back on the history of Israel, we see lots of compromises occur over time. These small compromises built up and led to the extensive wickedness that we see in Israel in the time of Jeroboam II.

Hosea 4:17 says that Israel had joined itself to idols. Hosea 6:9 depicts robbers and murderers throughout Israel. Hosea 6:10 says, "In the House of Israel I have seen a horrible thing." The wickedness of Israel is clearly on display. An interesting statement is made in Hosea 5:4, "Their deeds do not allow them / To return to their God."

This is an interesting statement considering the structure of Hosea, which keeps pointing back to God's promise of restoration for Israel. God said again and again that He would restore Israel to Himself, and they would be faithful to Him. But how does this work together with the statement made in Hosea 5:4?

We need to understand this statement in light of Israel's twisted thinking at this time. The salvation God promises and the restoration that will come to Israel will be completely a work of God. If left to their own devices Israel would only run further and further away from God. Their twisting of the truth corrupted their own thinking to such an extent that they were not able to turn back to God. God is the one who must work within them to change their hearts to bring them back to Himself. Deceit and lies are initially an attempt to get away with something or injure someone else. But in the end, as is the case with Israel, deceit ends up destroying the deceiver.

Faithfulness

The central theme of the book of Hosea is faithfulness. Israel was in covenant relationship with God. We can see all the way back in Exodus and Deuteronomy that the Israelites accepted the terms of the covenant. However, time and time again the people broke the covenant and rebelled against God.

Throughout all the Old Testament, and especially in Hosea, we see the contrast between the unfaithfulness of people and the faithfulness of God. In Hosea 6:4 God said, "What shall I do with you, O Ephraim? / What shall I do with you, O Judah? / For your loyalty is like a morning cloud / And like the dew which goes away early."

In this instance, Judah was indicted together with the northern kingdom of Israel in Hosea. This further lends support to the understanding that human faithfulness is fleeting in comparison with God's faithfulness. It is like a morning cloud which disappears as the sun rises.

The beautiful thing about God's faithfulness in the book of Hosea is that it is effectual. God was not just waiting patiently. God promised not only to be faithful in the covenant relationship, but to bring about the future faithfulness of Israel. God's faithfulness effects and changes the faithlessness of Israel. This is a beautiful picture of faithfulness that does not change even though the covenant partner gives every reason to abandon the covenant.

> "God is not man, that He should lie,
> Nor a son of man, that He should repent;
> Has He said, and will He not do it?
> Or has He spoken, and will He not make it good?"
>
> (Num. 23:19)

Reflection questions:

1. Why do you think God would command the marriage of Hosea and Gomer?
2. In what ways does the culture today downplay the importance of covenant faithfulness?
3. What is the relationship between faithfulness and truth? In other words, why do the two parties within a covenant need to correctly understand each other?
4. How does the structure of the book of Hosea point to the surety of Israel's future restoration?

12

Joel

IT IS EASIER TO PIN DOWN the time of the book of Hosea than it is the book of Joel. The book of Joel does not link itself with any king of Israel or Judah. For that reason, it's hard to determine the exact time of the book's writing. But Joel has great prominence among the twelve Minor Prophets. The book of Joel focuses on the coming day of the Lord. We see this theme throughout many of the Minor Prophets. It was also referenced in Hosea.

More than any other minor prophet, Joel gave reference to the coming day of the Lord. The book centers on judgment with a promise of future restoration. The book is addressed to both Judah and to the nations.

In contrast to Hosea whose recipients are clearly the northern kingdom of Israel, Joel focuses on the southern kingdom of Judah. The name Joel in Hebrew means "Yahweh is God." This is fitting for the book because the power of God is on display in the coming judgment. The emphasis is upon Yahweh as the almighty Judge and Ruler.

Structure

We can see clear division in the structure of Joel, dividing the book in half. The first half is from 1:1 to 2:17, focusing upon the coming day of the Lord in Judah. The second half of the book is from 2:18 through 3:21, which focuses on the day of the Lord against the nations and the restoration of Judah.

Chapter 1 describes a locust invasion of the land, which brings great desolation. Chapter 2 also speaks about an invasion, and it is not clear if this is the same invasion or a different one. However this invasion also brings great destruction, and the question is asked, "The day of the Lord is indeed great and very awesome, / And who can endure it?" (2:11).

Joel 2:12 begins a section that calls for the repentance of Judah and return to the Lord. Joel 2:18–28 prophesies spiritual renewal as well as the renewal of the land and blessing that God will reign down upon the people of Judah.

Joel 3 switches to speak God's judgment against the nations. The nations are depicted as violent and wicked, culminating in the battle against God in the Valley of Jehoshaphat, also known as the Valley of Jezreel. The structure of Joel can be seen in this breakdown:

Joel 1:1–12	The locust invasion
Joel 1:13–20	A call for repentance
Joel 2:1–11	The invasion of God's army
Joel 2:12–32	A call for repentance
Joel 2:12–17	"Return to Me"
Joel 2:18–27	Physical blessing and restoration
Joel 2:28–32	Spiritual blessing and restoration
Joel 3:1–16	God's judgment of the nations
Joel 3:17–21	The future of Judah

PURPOSE

The purpose of Joel clearly is to point to the coming day of the Lord. This day of the Lord brings judgment upon Judah but also ultimate restoration for Judah. The day of the Lord also brings about full and final judgment upon the nations, especially those that surround Israel. Tyre and Sidon are mentioned in Joel 3:4 as well as Egypt and Edom in Joel 3:19.

However the statement is made that all the nations will be judged in the Valley of Jehoshaphat (Joel 3:2). This Valley of Jehoshaphat is called the valley of decision in Joel 3:14, pointing to the complete judgment of God and deliverance for His people.

JOEL PURPOSE STATEMENT: The impending day of the Lord will bring final judgment upon the nations as well as judgment and restoration of Judah.

THEMES

The day of the Lord is described by several characteristics in Joel. Joel 1:15 is the first verse to mention the term "day of the LORD" in this book.

The description given is that the day of the Lord is near. It is described this way as well in chapter 2. It is depicted as though it is right at hand, ready to happen at any time. Chapter 1 links the day of the Lord with agricultural destruction brought by locusts. This is a locust invasion of the land that destroys everything in its path, leading to desolation and starvation.

Joel begins by asking, "Has *anything like* this happened in your days, / Or in your fathers' days?" This, apparently, was devastation on a scale that had not been seen before.

Joel 2:1–11 continues to describe this day of the Lord and gives further detail. The invasion in chapter 2 is now depicted as coming at the hands of a great and powerful force (Joel 2:2). Joel 2:3 says that fire devours before them. Behind them is a desolate wilderness, nothing escapes from them.

The picture is painted in Joel 2:4 that the appearance of this force is like horses, but they also leap on the tops of mountains and march in perfect order (Joel 2:7–8). The key rhetorical question is asked at the end of this section, "Who can endure [the day of the LORD]?"

With this terrifying statement made, Joel then switches to speak about future restoration for Judah. God is described as gracious and merciful, slow to anger and abounding in steadfast love.

This is not contradictory to what was said about God's coming judgment. God is a just Judge and brings condemnation on the wicked. But He calls sinners to repent and turn back to Him because He is a gracious God.

Chapter 2 is contrasted with the desolation of chapter 1. Chapter 2 speaks of God sending the early rain to replenish Judah, providing grain, wine, and new oil for them. Right after this promise of restoration comes the most famous passage in Joel, quoted by Peter in his sermon in Acts 2:17–21. God promises that He will pour out His spirit on His people. The sun shall be turned to darkness and the moon to blood before the great and awesome day of the Lord comes. God promises that everyone who calls on the name of the Lord will be saved.

At this point, the focus changes to the nations. God says He will enter into judgment against the nations in the Valley of Jehoshaphat, known later as the Valley of Megiddo. From this, we get the name Armageddon, which means "mountain of Megiddo."

Megiddo is a small city that sits atop a hill, overlooking this vast valley. The wickedness of the nations is put on display, and God calls the nations to come to war in this valley. The day of the Lord is depicted as the harvest of the nations in this battle. As God judges the nations, He is also depicted as the Refuge for His people in Joel 3:16.

As is the case with many prophetic books in the Old Testament, it can be difficult to determine exactly what the day of the Lord looks like. Much description is given, but sometimes it is difficult to pin down what the prophecy is portraying.

For example, do chapter 1 and chapter 2 of Joel depict the same invasion or a different invasion? Chapter 1 clearly speaks about locusts. But chapter 2 speaks about an army that is described as horses that bring fire and destruction in their wake.

It is important to note that the goal of Joel is not to give a complete and final description as to what the day of the Lord looks like. Instead, Joel warns of coming judgment. This is literal judgment and a literal warning against those who would rebel against God.

In the wake of this judgment is also the consistent and clear promise of the restoration of Judah. There is a future hope and restoration for Judah that cannot be taken away. Even though specific description is not given, we can still see the warning and judgment of God as well as the promise of restoration for the people of Judah.

Reflection questions:

1. In what way are the first and second books of the Minor Prophets a paradigm for understanding all the Minor Prophets? In other words, how do the themes of Hosea and Joel point to the heart of all of the Minor Prophets?

2. What are some of the key descriptions that we learn about the day of the Lord from the book of Joel?

3. Why do you think it is important that God both judges and restores Judah as depicted in the book of Joel?

4. What is the key difference between the judgment of Judah and the judgment of the nations in Joel?

13

Amos

AMOS WAS A CONTEMPORARY of Hosea. Compared with some of the other Minor Prophets, the beginning of Amos gives a good amount of description about when the prophecy was made and some of the events surrounding it. Amos himself was described as one of the shepherds of Tekoa.

Second Samuel 14 mentions a place named Tekoa. Joab, King David's military commander, had an unnamed woman from Tekoa present a case before King David in order to get Absalom brought back from exile. Tekoa is also the name of a person in First Chronicles 2:24 and 4:5.

Tekoa was about ten miles south of Jerusalem. It is just south of Bethlehem, so it is interesting that Amos is listed among the shepherds of Tekoa. In this similar region, the angelic announcement of the birth of the Messiah would come to shepherds near Bethlehem. It is also interesting to note that Amos was from south of Jerusalem, but he was sent as a prophet to the northern kingdom of Israel.

Amos and Hosea, within twelve Minor Prophets, spoke most prominently to the northern kingdom of Israel. Jonah was another prophet who had relation with the northern kingdom. But most of the Minor Prophets spoke to the southern kingdom of Judah.

In addition to describing Amos as a shepherd, the time frame of the prophecy is also given. Amos 1:1 says this occurred in the days of Uzziah, king of Judah, and in the days of Jeroboam, king of Israel. Both kings were also mentioned in Hosea. Amos and Hosea would have been contemporaries, giving prophecy at the same time, perhaps knowing each other.

The first verse of Amos says this prophecy was given two years before the earthquake. This same earthquake is also mentioned in Zechariah 14:5, which gives a future prophecy about a coming earthquake that will split the Mount of Olives in two. This verse says the inhabitants of Jerusalem will flee, "Just as they fled before the earthquake in the days of Uzziah king of Judah." We do not know when this earthquake occurred, but the description in Amos 1:1 puts the prophecy in the eighth century BC.

Structure

Within the structure of Hosea, many sections speak of the restoration of Israel. That is not the case with the Amos. Much of this small book speaks about coming judgment. The first portion of the book speaks judgment against various nations. The nations mentioned are Damascus, Philistia, Tyre, Edom, Ammon, and Moab. These are all nations immediately surrounding Israel, and they all, at some point, made war upon Israel. The text speaks of one judgment after another given against these nations.

It is interesting that Israel and Judah are the last two kingdoms in this list. In the structure of the book, they are lumped together with the rest of the nations.

In Amos 3–6, indictments are laid down against Israel, giving the reasons for the coming judgment. This changes in Amos 7:1–9:10, in which Amos receives several different visions, some with specific judgment. The first vision is like Joel in that God gave Amos a picture of locusts coming to eat the vegetation of the land.

The second vision was of fire that "consumed the great deep and began to consume the farm land" (Amos 7:4). The third vision was of a plumb line that God sent out into Israel to measure their perversity. A fourth vision was given specifically against the high priest of Bethel, whose name was Amaziah. He spoke against Amos, and so God proclaimed an edict against Amaziah. The fifth vision was of a basket of summer fruit, which pointed to a coming famine in Israel. The sixth vision was of the Lord standing beside the altar, speaking judgment against Israel.

It appears that all is lost in Amos, except for the last portion of the book. Amos 9:11–15 promises that God will raise Israel up again. Blessing is seen in the abundance of food, the king being raised up, and Israel "will not again be rooted out of from their land / Which I have given them" (9:15). The following shows the outlined structure:

Amos 1:1	Introduction
Amos 1:2–2:16	Judgment against the Nations
Amos 1:3–5	Judgment against Damascus
Amos 1:6–8	Judgment against Philistia
Amos 1:9–10	Judgment against Tyre
Amos 1:11–12	Judgment against Edom
Amos 1:13–15	Judgment against Ammon
Amos 2:1–3	Judgment against Moab

Amos 2:4–5	Judgment against Judah
Amos 2:6–16	Judgment against Israel
Amos 3:1–6:14	Oracles of judgment against Israel
Amos 7:1–9:10	Visions of judgment on Israel
Amos 9:11–15	The restoration of Israel

PURPOSE

The purpose of the book of Amos seems to be quite bleak. While Hosea gave instances of promised restoration, Amos did not paint as bright of a picture. However, Amos did point to the restoration of Israel at the end of the book. The purpose of Amos was to point to the coming judgment. This is seen as unavoidable judgment that was a response to the wickedness not only of Israel but also of nations that surround Israel.

AMOS PURPOSE STATEMENT: Even though Israel will be restored eventually, God's judgment against Israel and its surrounding nations is certain.

THEMES

It can be difficult to read a book like Amos and try to wrap our minds around the prophesied destruction. It can be hard for us to understand why this destruction and judgment is necessary. How does the character of God fit into these kinds of passages?

Even when speaking about the judgment of the nations, God said He would send fire against them. This is stated in each of the prophecies against the nations. The fire will "devour . . . strongholds" (Amos 1:4, 7, 10, 12, 14, 2:2, 5, ESV). This description emphasizes that there will not be any safety or security against the judgment of God. It will be comprehensive and complete.

Additional description is given of the judgment coming against Israel. This includes famine (4:6), lack of rain (4:7), blight and mildew (4:9), pestilence and war (4:10). At times, the description of the judgment is staccato:

> "So many dead bodies!"
>
> "They are thrown everywhere!"
>
> "Silence!" (8:3, ESV)

Throughout Amos, God repeated a statement: "You have not returned to me." The punishments that came upon Israel previously were viewed as chastisements, which were meant to lead Israel back to God, like the discipline of a child. However, Israel did not get the message. They did not repent nor return to God. The judgment against Israel as depicted in Amos was final and complete. This is what makes the restoration of Israel at the end of the book stand out. Reading through the beginning of Amos, we do not expect to see restoration, only the final nail in the coffin of Israel's rebellion.

The judgment is also linked to God's choosing of Israel. Amos 3:2 says, "You only have I chosen among all the families of the earth; / Therefore, I will punish you for all your iniquities."

Israel entered covenant with God while still having a rebellious heart, ensuring their coming punishment. Israel promised to do all that God commanded them. When they demonstrated their true nature, a wicked heart in rebellion against God, God responded according to His character. Amos 4:12 says, "Therefore thus I will do to you, O Israel; / Because I will do this to you, / Prepare to meet your God, O Israel!" The theme of Amos is that there is no escape from this judgment.

The reader of Amos expects the complete destruction of Israel. Not until Amos 9:8 do we see a hint of Israel's restoration. God says, "I will not totally destroy the house of Jacob." Verse 10 continues, "All the sinners of My people will die by the sword."

A sifting and culling of the people of Israel is foretold. All those within Israel who rebel against God will be fully and finally judged. However, there will be those in Israel who turn back to God. These will be restored and raised, never to be uprooted again (Amos 9:15). Never again will they rebel against God, pointing to the new heart promised by Isaiah and Jeremiah. God will grant them a new nature, a new heart, which does not turn from Him, worshiping in spirit and truth.

Reflection questions:

1. How is Amos similar to Hosea? How are the two dissimilar?

2. In what time period did Amos prophesy? What was happening in Israel and Judah at this time?

3. According to the purpose and structure of the book, why is it necessary that Amos only speaks about the restoration of Israel at the end of the book?

4. In Amos 1 and 2, what are the reasons God gives for the coming judgment against the nations mentioned? Is this different for Israel and Judah?

14

Obadiah

OBADIAH IS ONE OF THE shortest books of the Bible, but it should not be overlooked. These twenty-one verses have an important message. The name Obadiah in Hebrew means "Servant of Yahweh." In service to the call of Yahweh, Obadiah delivers a message to Edom, a rival nation of Israel.

The nation of Edom was descended from Esau, Jacob's twin brother. The sibling rivalry went all the way back to the birth of Jacob and Esau. The hatred between Israel and Edom had escalated to the point of war.

Edom is mentioned in many of the other prophetic books along with many other nations that surrounded Israel, nations that had long histories with Israel, just like Edom. Edom had a unique place because of the relationship between Jacob and Esau. The fact that Edom betrayed and went to war against Israel incited the Lord's anger. Not only was Edom prophesied against in this short book, but Obadiah also talked about the day of the Lord and the restoration of Israel.

Structure

This short book can be divided into two portions. The first half of the book is from verses 1 through 14, speaking about Edom being destroyed. Obadiah said in verse 7 that Edom had no understanding. Verse 8 also said the Lord would destroy the wise men of Edom.

Edom was known as a center for wisdom. It had a long history of sages and wise men who were famous for their wisdom. God turned this against them and said that while they had become proud in their wisdom, they actually did not have understanding. They would be cut off because their pride had brought them to ruin.

The second portion of this short book is from verses 15 through 21. This speaks of the day of the Lord, the restoration of Israel, and the fact that Israel would even possess the land of Edom. Verse 21 says the kingdom of

Edom would belong to the Lord. Obadiah has a simple structure that demonstrates the purpose of the book:

Obadiah 1–14	The destruction of Edom
Obadiah 15–21	The deliverance of Israel

PURPOSE

The purpose of Obadiah is to show the downfall of Edom, specifically because of Edom's lack of compassion for Israel and their violence against Israel. In contrast to this, the day of the Lord was emphasized, bringing the full and final restoration of Israel. Israel would inherit all that Edom once possessed.

OBADIAH PURPOSE STATEMENT: God will judge Edom because of her violence against Israel, but Israel will be delivered in the day of the Lord and possess the mountain of Esau.

THEMES

This short book is concerned primarily with the relationship between Edom and Israel. Israel was referred to as Jacob several times, emphasizing the previous sibling rivalry between Jacob and Esau. Judah was mentioned, and Israel was also referred to as the House of Joseph.

Edom was condemned for pride in verses 3 and 4. Starting in verse 10, Edom was also condemned for violence against Israel. Edom had rejoiced at the downfall of Israel and Judah. Though Edom was not the primary aggressor, they came on the heels of those who had conquered.

It is not clear from this short book which nation or nations conquered Israel. This might refer to the downfall of the northern kingdom in 722 BC. It is possible that it is also referring to the downfall of the southern kingdom of Judah in 586 BC. Or it may be referring to a previous war between Israel and another nation, such as Damascus, which predates the downfall of the northern kingdom of Israel. Unfortunately, we do not know exactly which conquest is being referred to. This makes the dating of Obadiah difficult. The prophecies against Edom are clear, but the historical context surrounding this indictment is unknown.

Psalm 137:7 says, "Remember, O LORD, against the sons of Edom / The day of Jerusalem, / Who said, 'Raze it, raze it / To its very foundation.'"

This is a helpful Biblical parallel, but not necessarily contemporary with Obadiah. One additional biblical parallel is Jeremiah 49:7–12. This text makes a lot of similar statements and parallel ideas to the first nine verses of Obadiah. But again, it is not clear if Jeremiah was pulling from Obadiah, if Obadiah was pulling from Jeremiah, if they were contemporaries or if they were just writing similar content.

It is important that the prophecy given against Edom calls for Edom's complete destruction. Verse 18 says, "'There will be no survivor of the house of Esau,' / For the LORD has spoken." Many other nations are spoken against in the Prophets, but only a few prophecies are made against nations for their complete and utter destruction.

As is common throughout the Minor Prophets, the fulfillment of this prophecy is linked with the day of the Lord. As verse 15 says, "The day of the LORD draws near on all the nations."

In all the Minor Prophets, the day of the Lord is depicted as being close at hand. This fulfillment of the day of the Lord will bring about punishment for other nations, destruction of some nations, and the full restoration of Israel. Obadiah specified that not only would Israel be restored, but they would also possess all the land of Edom, referred to as the mountain of Esau.

It is important as well to note that a few of the Minor Prophets seem to focus on nations outside of Israel, giving prophetic messages to these nations. However, even though a minor prophet may speak to another nation, the message is always tied back to Israel. God's fulfillment of His promises to Israel is always the theme and centerpiece of every book of the Minor Prophets.

Reflection questions:

1. Many nations are judged by God. Why do you think it is necessary that an entire book be dedicated to the judgment of Edom?

2. Many nations are judged by God, but only a handful will be destroyed with no survivors left. Why do you think Edom is in that category?

3. What new information do we get from Obadiah about the coming day of the Lord that we have not yet seen in other Minor Prophets?

15

JONAH

IT IS INTERESTING THAT Obadiah and Jonah are placed right next to each other within the Minor Prophets. Obadiah had a very negative message for a nation outside of Israel. Jonah was the opposite with a negative message against Israel but a positive message for the primary enemy of Israel, Assyria. Hosea was sent directly to the northern kingdom of Israel. Joel had a message for the southern kingdom of Judah. Amos was directed towards the northern kingdom of Israel. Obadiah mentioned both Israel and Judah, and it is difficult to know when Obadiah was written.

Jonah was directed against the northern kingdom of Israel, primarily because the message of Jonah was for the chief enemy of northern Israel. God showed Nineveh great mercy. The chief royal city of the empire of Assyria often changed with each new ruler. Nineveh, at the time of Jonah, was a prominent city, but it is not clear which ruler was presiding over the city.

Sennacherib, around the time of the fall of the northern kingdom of Israel, greatly extended Nineveh and built it up as his royal city. He redirected water from the northern mountains to water his lavish gardens within the city walls. But it is not clear who was ruling Nineveh at the time of Jonah, whether it was Sennacherib or someone else.

Jonah's name in Hebrew means "Dove," often used as a symbol for peace. This is ironic because Jonah only desired the destruction of Nineveh. He did everything he could to avoid delivering his message to the people of Nineveh. In contrast to the other Minor Prophets, Jonah is primarily written in a narrative format. The exception to this is Jonah's prayer in chapter 2. It is important for us to understand how the narrative and the structure demonstrate the purpose of the book.

STRUCTURE

The structure of Jonah is quite intricate. It is in a chiastic form, which means the book mirrors itself. A few other books are put in this structure, such as the book of Esther. An author selects this structure to emphasize the center point in the book.

In Jonah 1:1–2, God instructed Jonah to go preach to Nineveh, and He repeated this in Jonah 3:1–2. In Jonah 1:3, Jonah rejected God's command to preach to these Gentiles. In Jonah 3:3, Jonah accepted his commission. In Jonah 1:4, God demonstrated His power. In Jonah 3:4, God's plan was revealed to Nineveh.

The center point of the book is the fish vomiting Jonah onto dry land (Jon. 2:10). This center point is seen after the prayer of Jonah, demonstrating the compassion of God on Jonah, an Israelite. The compassion of God is on display throughout the entire book. Jonah desired that God's compassion only be shown to Israel, not to Israel's enemies. The full structure can be seen in this diagram:

Jonah 1:1–2	God sends Jonah
Jonah 1:3	Jonah rejects his call
Jonah 1:4	God reveals His power
Jonah 1:5–16	The sailors submit to God
Jonah 1:17	God rescues Jonah
Jonah 2:1–9	Jonah's prayer
Jonah 2:10	The fish vomits Jonah out
Jonah 3:1–2	God sends Jonah
Jonah 3:3	Jonah accepts his call
Jonah 3:4	God reveals His plan
Jonah 3:5–10	Nineveh submits to God
Jonah 4:1–3	Jonah complains of God's mercy
Jonah 4:4–11	Jonah's lesson

Identifying this structure helps us understand the purpose of the book. We can see God rescuing Jonah and showing him mercy, but Jonah complained of God showing mercy to the Ninevites. We can also see the contrast between Jonah's prayer in chapter 2, which is a prayer of worship to God, and the simple lesson that Jonah needed to learn in chapter 4 of God's sovereignty and God's compassion. The center point of the book is Jonah's second chance. God showed Jonah mercy by delivering him from drowning. This is the turning point of the book. The expectation was that Jonah's character would change from being one who had no compassion and did not follow God's commands to one who understood God's compassion and was ready to show that compassion to the Ninevites.

A key point of the structure is that the book leaves the reader hanging. We do not ever learn if Jonah repented of his hard-heartedness. The book ends with God's statement concerning His compassion. We do not know how Jonah responded to God's statement. In a sense, it's an open-ended book that asks the question of whether the reader will be compassionate, whether Israel will be compassionate and fulfill its mandate from God.

Purpose

The book of Jonah sheds light on the mission of God. Several places in the Old Testament point to the plan of God for the salvation of the Gentiles. The Old Testament is not only about the salvation of Israel. Israel was meant to be a light to the Gentiles.

This is seen in other places of the Old Testament such as in Psalm 67. Part of the reason God selected Israel out of all the nations was that Israel might be transformed and thus bring the good news to the rest of the world. However, throughout their whole history they did not accomplish this task.

We see glimpses of this throughout the Old Testament, such as when the Queen of Sheba visited Solomon after hearing of his great wisdom. But on the whole, Israel failed in their mission to show God's compassion and character to the Gentile nations. Instead of being missionaries, Israel became like the nations around them, worshipping idols and following their own desires.

Jonah is a pinnacle portion of the Old Testament, and indeed of the Minor Prophets, in showing the missional attitude of God. No random nation was selected to demonstrate God's compassion to the Gentiles. God chose to show compassion to Israel's worst enemy. This points to the purpose of the book that all nations are to be reached, not just the nations that would be friendly to Israel.

The purpose of Jonah is also to show the hard-heartedness of Israel, as exemplified by the prophet Jonah. As we clearly see in the text, Jonah did everything he could to avoid God's compassion being shown to the Ninevites.

Jonah's hatred and stubbornness compelled him to act contrary to God's missional attitude. Jonah is seen as an exemplar of Israel in this way. Though Jonah's prayer in chapter 2 was worshipful, on the whole Jonah was a negative character in the book. The purpose of the book is to contrast God's intended purpose with the hard-heartedness of Israel.

> **Jonah Purpose Statement:** Even though Israel was hard-hearted in their mission to be a light to the nations, God still showed compassion to repentant Gentiles.

Themes

The story of Jonah is one of the most recognized of all the Minor Prophets. This story of the great fish and Jonah has been told in Sunday schools for generations.

Often, the story of Jonah in the belly of the fish overshadows the purpose and themes of the book. We are not even sure what kind of fish swallowed Jonah. It is often depicted as a giant whale. But the words in Hebrew are just "a great fish."

Many have argued about whether Jonah could have survived in the belly of the fish. At times there have been accounts of other people being swallowed whole by a large fish or a whale. But whether other stories exist or not, the text of Jonah portrays this at face value. The narrative is straightforward and should be taken as such. Jonah surviving in the belly of the fish for three days is a miracle on par with the many miracles described in the Old Testament.

Jesus spoke of Jonah in the Gospel of Matthew. In Matthew 12:39–40, Jesus said the sign that would be given to the hard-hearted Jewish leaders was the sign of Jonah. Jesus explained that just as Jonah was in the belly of the fish for three days and three nights, so Jesus would be in the tomb for three days and three nights.

Jesus spoke of the historicity of this account of Jonah, and we should also take the story at face value. More important than debating whether the fish could have swallowed Jonah, we need to understand the purpose of the book and its themes. The purpose of the book emphasizes God's compassion, and this book clearly demonstrates God's sovereignty.

God is sovereign over nature, sending a great storm upon the sea. We can parallel this event with Jesus calming the sea in the Gospels. Both accounts demonstrate God as the Creator. God appointed the great fish to swallow Jonah, and God also commanded the fish to vomit Jonah back out.

In chapter 4, God appointed a plant to grow as shade over Jonah's head, and God also appointed a worm the very next day to destroy the plant.

Then, God appointed a scorching east wind to beat down on Jonah. Jonah did not question whether God was able to do these things or not. Jonah did not question whether God would show mercy to the Ninevites. Jonah recognized God's sovereignty; Jonah recognized God's compassion. But Jonah still disobeyed God.

Reflection questions:

1. Why was Jonah so hard-hearted against the Ninevites?
2. In how many ways does God demonstrate His compassion and mercy in the book of Jonah?
3. Why should the book of Jonah be viewed as a historical account?
4. How does the book of Jonah end, and what does this tell us about the purpose of the book?
5. Would you say that Jonah is a good character or a bad character? Why or why not?

16

Micah

SOME CONTEXT IS GIVEN at the beginning of this Minor Prophet. We can first see that the name Micah means in Hebrew, "Who is like Yahweh." It is related to the name Michael, which means "Who is like God."

The text says this Micah was from a place called Moresheth. In verse 14, we gain a little bit of clarity with this place because it is called Moresheth-Gath. Jeremiah 26:18 says Micah was a prophet from Moresheth in the days of Hezekiah, king of Judah.

These are the only times this place name is mentioned. The only hint we get of the location is the link it has with Gath. Of course, the most famous person from Gath was Goliath, but perhaps Micah should be the most famous person from this area.

Micah's message was one full of wonder and hope for Israel. Micah prophesied during the days of Jotham, Ahaz, and Hezekiah, kings of Judah. This would have been from the middle of the eighth century to the beginning of the seventh century BC.

While no kings of northern Israel are mentioned, verse 1 says Micah saw this prophecy concerning Samaria and Jerusalem. By the time of Jesus, Samaria was linked with the Samaritans, enemies of the Jews. But long before this, Samaria was a city built by King Omri of the northern kingdom of Israel, toward the beginning of the ninth century BC.

Omri was the father of King Ahab. Omri established the dynasty of Omri and was well-known throughout the area as a powerful king. This was the capital city of northern Israel until the Assyrians destroyed it in 722 BC.

The book of Micah opens by saying that the prophecy given to Micah concerned both Samaria and Jerusalem, the two capital cities of the northern and southern kingdoms. During the reign of Ahaz in Judah, Samaria in the northern kingdom of Israel was destroyed. So, Micah's prophetic career spanned the destruction of the northern kingdom.

It is interesting to note that the two capital cities were highlighted. This is further explained in Micah 1:5, which says, "All this is for the rebellion of Jacob / And for the sins of the house of Israel. / What is the rebellion of Jacob? / Is it not Samaria? / What is the high place of Judah? / Is it not Jerusalem?"

These two capital cities were seen as the leaders in the rebellion against God. Micah was sent directly to them to proclaim the word of the Lord.

STRUCTURE

The structure of the book helps demonstrate the purpose behind Micah's writing. Like many of the other Minor Prophets, the structure of Micah is seen in cycles of judgment and restoration. After the introduction of verse 1, the first of these cycles began.

This first cycle emphasized God's judgment of both Israel and Judah with Samaria and Jerusalem at the lead. This continued until the end of chapter 2. After this, the second cycle began in chapter 3, going to the end of chapter 5.

God specifically focused on the leaders, denouncing them for their hypocrisy, greed, and wickedness. These wicked leaders were depicted as those "Who eat the flesh of my people, / Strip off their skin from them, / Break their bones / And chop *them* up as for the pot" (Mic. 3:3). Instead of sacrificially leading, they devoured the people for their own greed.

The third cycle began in chapter 6 and continued to the end of the book. This third cycle focused on God's indictment against the people.

Each of these cycles began with the declaration of judgment. Each of these cycles also ended with a statement of restoration. This is seen in the last two verses of chapter 2, in chapters 4 and 5, and in Micah 7:7–20. The structure of the book can be outlined:

- Micah 1:1 — Introduction
- Micah 1:2–2:13 — The first cycle
  - Micah 1:2–2:11 — Judgment against Israel and Judah
  - Micah 2:12–13 — Future restoration of the nation
- Micah 3:1–5:15 — The second cycle
  - Micah 3:1–12 — Judgment against the leaders
  - Micah 4:1–5:15 — Future restoration of leadership
- Micah 6:1–7:20 — The third cycle
  - Micah 6:1–7:6 — Judgment of the people
  - Micah 7:7–20 — Future restoration of the people

Purpose

In the structure of Micah, the central focus of the book is on the future restoration of leadership. This includes the most famous text in Micah, "But as for you, Bethlehem Ephrathah, / *Too* little to be among the clans of Judah, / From you One will go forth for Me to be ruler in Israel. / His goings forth are from long ago, / From the days of eternity" (Mic. 5:2).

This is the prophecy of the Messiah coming from Bethlehem, fulfilled in the Gospels with Jesus. Micah continued to describe this Messiah, saying that He would be the peace of Israel. He would be a deliverer from those who oppressed Israel. Micah clearly portrayed God's judging Israel, but just as we saw with Hosea, restoration was promised again and again.

> **Micah Purpose Statement:** Though God will judge Israel and Judah for their sin, God will send His Messiah, who will restore the nation.

Themes

Micah put the sins of Israel on display. Samaria and Jerusalem were seen as the leaders in the wickedness against God. Chapter 1 speaks about the idolatry within Israel. The oppressors were also condemned in chapter 2. These were the ones who devised wickedness, coveted and seized others' possessions, and oppressed the poor.

The leaders were described in chapter 3 as devouring the people. Among this group were the false prophets seen in Micah 3:5. Micah 6:12 says, "For the rich men of *the* city are full of violence, / Her residents speak lies, / And their tongue is deceitful in their mouth."

The destruction to come upon Israel was painted with bleak colors. But there is no injustice with God. Just as we have seen in many of the other Minor Prophets, the depiction of Israel's wickedness was great. Their judgment was just and deserved.

As with many of the other Minor Prophets, the theme that goes along with the sin of Israel and subsequent judgment was the mercy and kindness of God. As seen in the purpose statement, this was especially on display in the promise of the coming Messiah.

Micah gave specific details of this coming Messiah. The New Testament pointed to this as evidence of the Messiah being Jesus. This description was certainly seen in chapter 5, but the Messiah was also seen in other passages. Micah 2:12–13 speaks about the king who would lead the people. Micah 7:14 speaks about the leader as a shepherd.

If the Minor Prophets only had description of sin and judgment, they would be bleak indeed. But in these windows of hope we see promises of restoration and details of God's future plans for Israel. Micah, more than any other minor prophet other than Zechariah, perhaps, gives us the most specific detail of the coming Messiah.

A final important note concerning Micah is the emphasis placed upon the mountain of the Lord. Micah 4 is similar to Isaiah 2. Both have similar wording, and both describe the mountain of the Lord.

Micah 4 places this description in the "latter days." The mountain of the Lord is linked with the house of the Lord in Micah 4:1. Micah said every single nation would come to this mountain of the Lord, to the house of God. Everyone who comes is searching to learn the ways of God. Micah 4:2 says, "For from Zion will go forth the law, / Even the word of the LORD from Jerusalem."

God will sit as judge on this mountain. Justice will go forth from this mountain. The character of God will be on display from this mountain. God promises that the destitute and despised will be gathered together, and God will reign over them from Mount Zion. The once-powerful nations will come in humility to this mountain to learn the ways of God.

Both Micah and Isaiah emphasized this theme in their writings. We must link together the idea of a ruling Messiah with the kingdom from which He rules, known as the mountain that is the highest of all mountains, to which all the people come (Mic. 4:1).

Reflection questions:

1. Where in the New Testament is Micah 5:2 quoted, and what is the context?
2. Why are Samaria and Jerusalem specifically addressed in the introduction to Micah?
3. What is the mountain of the House of the Lord, and what is its importance for the last days? Why do all nations come to this mountain?

17

Nahum

THE NAME NAHUM IN Hebrew means "comforter." This is interesting because this short Minor Prophet has nothing comforting to say to Assyria. The prophecy concerns Nineveh, according to verse 1, with Nineveh as the capital city and representation of the entire Assyrian Empire.

Assyria, of course, was the empire that destroyed the northern kingdom of Israel. Assyria was overthrown by the Babylonian Empire, who later destroyed the southern kingdom of Judah in 586 BC.

Nahum was from a place called Elkosh, which is difficult to locate. Some have argued that Elkosh was near Galilee, but no definitive proof has come to light. We do not know how long after Jonah that Nahum was written.

The city of Nineveh responded positively to Jonah's preaching. Even the king of Nineveh repented before God. But by the time Nahum was written Nineveh was depicted as corrupt, wicked, prideful, and full of violence.

How long would it have taken for this change to happen within Nineveh? We do not know. But the grace that was shown to Nineveh did not result in Nineveh's perpetual godliness.

Structure

The structure of this short book is quite straightforward. The three chapters demonstrate the three major portions of the book. Chapter 1 speaks of the nature of God as One who will have vengeance upon His adversaries. Chapter 2 speaks of the destruction of Nineveh. Chapter 3 is a lament that concerning the fall of Nineveh. This lament of chapter 3 is similar to the lament for Babylon in Revelation 18. The layout of the structure is seen below:

Nahum 1:1	Introduction
Nahum 1:2–15	God's Avenging Character
Nahum 2:1–13	The Destruction of Nineveh
Nahum 3:1–19	The Lament for Nineveh

Purpose

The purpose of the book of Nahum is also quite straightforward. We should see the purpose in light of Assyria's conquest of Israel. It is not just that Nineveh would be destroyed. The reason why Nineveh was destroyed was because God was avenging their conquest of Israel. Their wickedness was on full display, and God proclaimed that He would humble them.

> **Nahum Purpose Statement:** Because of Assyria's pride and conquest of Israel, God will utterly destroy Nineveh.

Themes

The focus of Nahum is the destruction of Nineveh. The metaphors used to paint this picture are interesting. Assyria took great pride in their military might. Their armies ruled for generations.

Nahum depicted Assyria's armies as now being worthless. Nahum 3:17 said the princes of Assyria were like grasshoppers that had flown away. Nahum 1:12 says, "Though they are at full *strength* and likewise many, / Even so, they will be cut off and pass away."

In addition, Assyria boasted of its great building projects and palaces. Sennacherib built his palace in Nineveh and named it "The palace without a rival." In contrast to this, Nahum 2:6 said, "The gates of the rivers are opened / And the palace is dissolved."

Sennacherib spent more than a decade building canals to divert water from the mountains in the north down to Nineveh to water his lavish gardens. On these canals that he built, he inscribed all manner of titles for himself. He had his slaves carve out along the length of these canals how great he was and how great were the gods that he served. One of the titles that he gave to himself was "king of the universe."

Sennacherib was one in a line of many boastful and arrogant rulers of Assyria. Sennacherib's grandson, Ashurbanipal, was the last great ruler of Assyria before its destruction by the Babylonians.

Ashurbanipal is depicted in the "lion reliefs," which are seen in the British Museum today. In these reliefs, Ashurbanipal performs an annual ritual that was done near Nineveh. As king, he would kill a whole group of uncaged lions to demonstrate his power and kingly might. It was the king's responsibility to maintain and rule over the lions, which were a symbol of Assyrian might. Nahum 2:11 asks, "Where is the den of the lions?" The lions, the symbol of the pride and power of Assyria, are no more. God has turned against them, and Nahum says, "A sword will devour your young lions" (Nah. 2:13).

The metaphors throughout this little book pinpoint the arrogance and pride that Nineveh had. Assyria represented generations of rulers and generations of people who opposed God. Though Jonah was a bright light amid this, Assyria, throughout the Old Testament, was seen as the archenemy of Israel. God promised to bring them to an end, a promise that was fulfilled in the conquest of Assyria by Babylon.

Reflection questions:

1. Why is it necessary that an entire book be dedicated to the prophecy of the destruction of Nineveh?
2. What metaphors can you find in Nahum? How do these help explain the purpose of the book?
3. Read Nahum 1:15. How does this verse fit into the purpose of Nahum?

18

Habakkuk

THIS SHORT BOOK OF the Minor Prophets is unique in that Habakkuk made complaints that were followed by answers from God. This determines the structure of the book.

We are able to see the time frame of the book because of the mention of the Chaldeans. "Chaldeans" is another term for the Babylonians, who destroyed the southern kingdom of Judah in 586 BC. Specifically, in 586 BC the temple of Solomon was destroyed. Habakkuk 1:6 says, "For behold, I am raising up the Chaldeans, / That fierce and impetuous people / Who march throughout the earth / To seize dwelling places which are not theirs."

This prophecy concerning the Chaldeans places the oracle of Habakkuk after the fall of the northern kingdom of Israel. Only after the fall of the northern kingdom did the Babylonians truly come to power, destroying the Assyrian Empire and becoming the dominant empire in the region.

Again, we can follow the Minor Prophets generally chronologically. Hosea seemed to be early in comparison, certainly before the fall of the northern kingdom. And Malachi, at the end of the Minor Prophets, is certainly a post-exilic book, meaning it was written after Judah returned from the Babylonian exile back to the land. Habakkuk lamented the fact that the Chaldeans had risen to power and were oppressing the southern kingdom of Judah.

It is difficult for us to understand how God would use a pagan nation to punish Israel. Habakkuk had the same difficulty with this idea. Like Jonah, Habakkuk had no love for Israel's enemies. Jonah responded in a wicked way, unwilling to preach the good news to the capital city of Nineveh.

Habakkuk asked a similar question as to how God could use the Chaldeans, a pagan and idolatrous nation, to punish the nation of Israel. Though Israel rebelled against God, at the very least, they were God's chosen people. The Babylonians were pagan people who wholeheartedly worshipped a whole host of different gods.

Structure

Habakkuk reads in a similar way to some of the psalms. When we think of prophecy, we often think of books like Ezekiel and Joel, which can be difficult to understand because of the imagery that they use.

Habakkuk has some imagery, but the book reads more like a prayer rather than a prophet. We can see the structure clearly in the complaints and prayers that Habakkuk has, followed by the answers that the Lord gives. The structure of the book itself is not difficult to see; the difficulty is in understanding the theology and the content of the book. This again goes back to the question of how God can use a wicked nation to punish Judah. The following is the structure of the book:

Habakkuk 1:1	Introduction
Habakkuk 1:2–11	The first cycle
Habakkuk 1:2–4	Habakkuk's first complaint
Habakkuk 1:5–11	God's response
Habakkuk 1:12–2:20	The second cycle
Habakkuk 1:12–2:1	Habakkuk's second complaint
Habakkuk 2:2–2:20	God's response
Habakkuk 3:1–19	Habakkuk's prayer
Habakkuk 3:1–2	Habakkuk's request
Habakkuk 3:3–16	Habakkuk's praise
Habakkuk 3:17–19	Habakkuk's rejoicing

Purpose

If a single verse could be listed as the purpose of Habakkuk, it would be Habakkuk 2:4. We will look at this verse more in the next section, but its emphasis is that the righteous shall live by faith. This is the issue Habakkuk was dealing with. He did not know why the wicked were prevailing and growing stronger and oppressing God's people. He cried his questions out to God to try to understand.

The key point of the book is that the righteous one relies on God and sees God as the One who provides the answers. The righteous person puts his or her hope in God even if wickedness flourishes all around.

Habakkuk Purpose Statement: The righteous will live by faith, trusting in the sovereign God who plans all things according to the counsel of His will.

Themes

A few portions of the Old Testament deal with theodicy. Theodicy is the question of how can sin and wickedness exist in a world that was created by a righteous God. Of course, the book of Job is the key text that deals with this question. But Habakkuk also interacts with this question. Habakkuk asks how God can make use of wickedness for His own purposes.

We need to see this in light of the historicity of the text. When Habakkuk spoke about the Chaldeans coming against Israel, he was speaking about great armies destroying, murdering, plundering, and doing unspeakable things against his own people, God's chosen people.

This is not a question in isolation that is thought of by philosophers and debated by skeptics. This is a real-world, real-life question that Habakkuk struggled with.

In many of the other Minor Prophets, we don't see the thinking or reasoning of the prophet himself. Instead, the prophet is a mouthpiece of God, giving the oracles of God. We don't necessarily hear the prayers or read the prophet's thoughts. We do see Jonah's rebellion and Jonah's heart attitude. But that is not as common among the Minor Prophets.

Habakkuk cried out against the destruction that he saw coming. We must remember this is the oracle of Habakkuk, so he was seeing what God would bring against Judah before it happened. He saw destruction and violence that would sweep across Judah and Jerusalem by the hand of the Chaldeans. Habakkuk 1:4 says, "For the wicked surround the righteous; / Therefore justice comes out perverted." Habakkuk was asking how there could be justice through a wicked instrument.

To help answer this question, the book of Habakkuk emphasizes the inscrutable ways of God. This begins in verse 5 of chapter 1 with the statement from God, "Look among the nations! Observe! / Be astonished! Wonder! / Because *I am* doing something in your days— / You would not believe if you were told."

Habakkuk emphasized the fact that God's ways are unknowable. The difficulty that Habakkuk had was being forced to rely upon God without knowing all the details of God's plan. Habakkuk did not comprehend what God was doing, so the beginning of the book shows us he struggled with trusting in God. In 1:12, Habakkuk recognized that God had established the Chaldeans as a judgment against Israel. It is also important to see that Habakkuk remembered there was no wickedness or evil within God. This is seen in 1:13 as well as throughout the book.

Habakkuk pointed to the Chaldeans' idolatry. He gave an example of a fisherman who throws his net into the sea, collects fish, and drags them from the water. After he drags them out of the water, "Therefore they offer a sacrifice to their net / And burn incense to their fishing net; / Because through these things their catch is large, / And their food is plentiful" (Hab. 1:16).

He pointed to the absurdity of this, but this is exactly what the Chaldeans did in their idolatry. Habakkuk 2:18 also points to this when it says, "What profit is the idol when its maker has carved it, / *Or* an image, a teacher of falsehood? / For *its* maker trusts in his own handiwork / When he fashions speechless idols!"

In contrast to idolatry, God was the One who was orchestrating all of history. Habakkuk was trying to understand how God could use the idolater to humble "those more righteous than they" (1:13).

The apostle Paul pulled from this issue in his letter to the Romans. The letter to the Romans is a beautiful theological work with the sovereignty of God and the faith of the righteous one as its centerpiece. After Paul gave his greeting to the Romans and spoke of his desire to visit Rome, he gave his thesis statement for the book. His thesis statement was not something he came up with on his own. Rather, his thesis statement was a quotation from Habakkuk 2:4: "The righteous *man* shall live by faith" (Rom. 1:17).

Habakkuk 2:4 is situated within one of the answers God gave to Habakkuk. This statement comes on the heels of Habakkuk's second complaint, in which he asked how God could use an idolatrous people to punish His chosen nation. Within the answer that God gave to Habakkuk, verse 4 says, "Behold, as for the proud one, / His soul is not right within him; / But the righteous will live by his faith."

This is the contrast made between the truly wicked unbeliever and the one who fears God. Habakkuk was an example of someone who feared God, someone who loved God, who was still questioning how God was working in the world. The distinction between an unbeliever and a believer is that the believer, like Habakkuk, submits himself to God, trusting in the character of God even if the details of how God is working are not known.

Habakkuk was reminded of all of this in chapter 3, which was his prayer to God. In verse 2, he reiterated that he feared God. Habakkuk reiterated that God was sovereign. Not only was God sovereign, but He also orchestrated the salvation of His people, seen in 3:13.

Habakkuk made a stirring statement in 3:16, "Because I must wait quietly for the day of distress, / For the people to arise *who* will invade us."

Habakkuk didn't know when or how, but he relied upon the character of God, knowing that God would bring about justice. Habakkuk ends with this statement similar to Job 1:21.

> Though the fig tree should not blossom
> And there be no fruit on the vines,
> *Though* the yield of the olive should fail
> And the fields produce no food,
> Though the flock should be cut off from the fold
> And there be no cattle in the stalls,
> Yet I will exult in the LORD;
> I will rejoice in the God of my salvation.
> The Lord GOD is my strength,
> And He has made my feet like hinds' *feet*,
> And makes me walk on my high places.
>
> (Hab. 3:17–19)

Reflection questions:

1. In what ways have you struggled with the question of evil? Do you find yourself sympathizing with Habakkuk's questions and struggles to understand?
2. Why do you think Habakkuk found it necessary to emphasize the sovereignty of God throughout this short book?
3. In what way is Habakkuk 2:4 a thesis statement for this book? And how does Paul use it as a centerpiece for his letter to the Romans?

19

Zephaniah

ZEPHANIAH, IN LIKE manner as Habakkuk, focused on Judah. Some details are given about Zephaniah and the time when he wrote. His prophetic career was during the days of Josiah, king of Judah.

Josiah was the grandson of Manasseh, one of the most wicked kings of Judah. Manasseh was succeeded by his son Amon, who was also a wicked king. Josiah was only eight years old when he came to the throne, and several godly leaders in Judah influenced him. A reform took place during the days of Josiah, and this was when Zephaniah was prophesying.

Even though this reform under Josiah took place in Judah, Zephaniah begins with a statement of coming judgment on Judah. Like several other Minor Prophets, Zephaniah emphasized the day of the Lord.

The book also ends with an important section in chapter 3 on the future restoration of Israel. In this way, Zephaniah had a lot of parallel themes to Joel, even though Joel was written to the northern kingdom of Israel.

Structure

The structure of the book can be broken into two major sections. The first section deals with the coming day of the Lord. The second section deals with Jerusalem, speaking both about judgment upon this city and future blessing. The structure of the book can be seen:

- Zephaniah 1:1 — Introduction
- Zephaniah 1:2–3:8 — Coming Judgment
  - Zephaniah 1:2–6 — Judgment of Idolators
  - Zephaniah 1:7–18 — The Coming Day of the Lord
  - Zephaniah 2:1–15 — Judgment on Judah's Enemies
  - Zephaniah 3:1–8 — Judgment of the Rebellious

Zephaniah 3:9–20	The Blessing of the Remnant
Zephaniah 3:9–10	Conversion of the Nations
Zephaniah 3:11–13	The Remnant of Israel
Zephaniah 3:14–20	The Restoration of Israel

Purpose

Many of the Minor Prophets speak about the coming day of the Lord. Zephaniah focuses on the purification of Israel and the surrounding nations in the day of the Lord. This purification is brought about by the culling of the rebellious from those who truly worship God.

It is important to see how the other nations were spoken of in Zephaniah, whether in terms of their future worship of God, or in terms of their destruction because of their rebellion. But Judah was still the central focus of the book.

> **Zephaniah Purpose Statement:** God will purify Israel and the nations in the coming day of the Lord by separating between the wicked and the righteous, destroying the wicked and restoring the righteous.

Themes

A key theme we see throughout Zephaniah is the searching of the Lord. God is depicted as One who is going throughout all of Judah looking for those who are rebellious.

The Lord declared that He would punish the wicked on the day when He comes (Zeph. 1:8–9). Zephaniah 1:12 also says, "It will come about at that time / That I will search Jerusalem with lamps, / And I will punish the men / Who are stagnant in spirit, / Who say in their hearts, / 'The LORD will not do good or evil!'"

We might link the philosophy of deism to this statement. Those who would say the Lord will not do good or ill are those who think God doesn't care and is not involved in the affairs of humanity.

But we should also understand this statement in light of the fear of God. Those who say the Lord will not do good or bad are those who do not fear any coming judgment. These people think that they can do whatever they want because God is not watching and does not care.

Not only did God rebuke this thinking, but in Judah, God promised that He would come destroy those who think this way. In 1:18, God said that no amount of wealth could deliver these people.

God is depicted as searching through all of Judah, punishing those who would rebel against Him. Toward the end of the book God made this statement:

> But I will leave among you
> A humble and lowly people.
> And they will take refuge in the name of the Lord.
> The remnant of Israel will do no wrong
> And tell no lies,
> Nor will a deceitful tongue
> Be found in their mouths.
>
> (Zeph. 4:12–13)

Zephaniah portrays God as One who would cull through Judah, destroying the wicked and saving the humble. A beautiful picture is painted for those left after this judgment. Israel was restored, and no one could make them afraid again.

Zephaniah 3:17 says, "The Lord your God is in your midst, / A victorious warrior. / He will exult over you with joy, / He will be quiet in His love, / He will rejoice over you with shouts of joy."

An additional note to make about Zephaniah is the inclusion of other nations. When God spoke about judgment, He primarily spoke about judgment upon Israel. But chapter 2 speaks about judgment upon nations that surround Israel, including Philistia, Moab, Cush, and Assyria.

When God spoke about blessing to Israel, there was also the mention of blessing to the nations, a conversion of the nations. Zephaniah 3:9–10 says that Gentiles from beyond the "rivers of Ethiopia" would be worshippers of God, bringing offerings to God. While the Minor Prophets focus their attention upon Israel and Judah, we should not forget the inclusion of the other nations.

Reflection questions:

1. How is the day of the Lord described in Zephaniah?

2. In what way is what is said to the nations parallel to what is said to Judah?

3. List out the descriptions that are given for the restoration of Israel (e.g., Zephaniah 3:15 says that God will be in the midst of His people).

20

Haggai

THE TONE OF THIS short book of Haggai is similar to Jonah in that Haggai is comprised of narrative. Also, several time references are given. The book begins with a time stamp of the second year of Darius the king in the sixth month on the first day of the month. This is when the word of the Lord came to Zerubbabel by the hand of Haggai.

Zerubbabel was the key leader who brought the Jews back from captivity in Babylon. Zerubbabel was descended directly through David's line. God sent the prophetic word of Haggai to Zerubbabel as the leader of the people. The message of Haggai concerned the Temple. God chastised the people for returning to the land and building their own houses, leaving the Temple in ruins.

The second year of Darius, the Persian king, would have been 520 BC. We can also trace the Jewish calendar to see that the first day of the sixth month would have been August 29. Over the course of the next few months, the word of the Lord came by the hand of Haggai to the people.

Time references are given throughout Haggai from August, 520 BC through December, 520 BC. Haggai the prophet was also mentioned in Ezra 5:1 and Ezra 6:14 in conjunction with Zechariah the prophet. Haggai, Zechariah, and Malachi were all well-known prophets in the post-exilic period.

Other important names during this time would have been Zerubbabel, who was the political leader; Joshua, the son of Jehozadak, the chief priest; Ezra, the scribe; and Nehemiah. Each played a specific role in the return of the exiles from Persia. Remember the Babylonians took Judah into exile, but while the Jews were in exile, Babylon was overthrown and replaced by the Medes and Persians.

Structure

It is most straightforward to see the structure of Haggai based on the time stamps given. Little is said about Haggai as a person. He was seen as the mouthpiece of God. The first time that Haggai brought a message was recorded in Haggai 1:1–11. In this message, God rebuked the people for spending their time building their own houses and not rebuilding the Temple. The next section of this book covered the response of the people, which was obedience (1:12–15).

The next section included the word of the Lord coming again to Zerubbabel through Haggai. The Temple being built was dwarfed in comparison to the glory of Solomon's temple. Everyone was aware of this. But God promised that the coming glory of the Temple would be greater even than Solomon's temple.

After this, starting in Haggai 2:10, the people were rebuked for not having their priorities straight. God promised that He would bless the people with abundance if they focused on Him wholeheartedly.

The final section, beginning in Haggai 2:20, seems to stand apart from the rest of the book. This was a specific message to Zerubbabel, whom God said would be His signet ring. God encouraged Zerubbabel that He would greatly exult Him. This was based on God's promise to David that his throne would endure forever. The structure of Haggai can be seen below:

Haggai 1:1–1:11	Rebuke for not building the Temple
Haggai 1:12–15	The people respond in obedience
Haggai 2:1–9	The coming glory of the Temple
Haggai 2:10–19	Rebuke and promise of blessing
Haggai 2:20–23	Zerubbabel will be the signet ring

PURPOSE

The focus of Haggai is on the Temple, but as is always the case in the Minor Prophets, we also need to see the focus on the hearts of the people. The people were rebuked because they did not have the right priorities.

This is an encouraging book because it speaks to the great blessing God promises to rain down on the people. The purpose of the book was not just to get the people working on the temple. Rather, it was to help the people have right priorities and be dedicated to God.

> **HAGGAI PURPOSE STATEMENT:** The Jews were to rebuild the Temple and dedicate themselves to God so that God would bless them and their leader.

THEMES

Several times throughout this short book, the people were called to consider their ways. They had spent time building their own houses, which would be a natural response to just returning from exile. Nothing was wrong with someone building their own house, but God asked the people to consider their own motivations and attitudes. They had been more concerned with their physical comfort than with the rebuilding of the Temple.

God even called the people to rebuild the Temple before they rebuilt the wall for their own defenses. The Temple was to be the highest priority as a demonstration of the people's commitment to God.

We see the word "consider" used throughout this short book. Haggai 1:5 says, "Consider your ways!" This was also said in Haggai 1:7. Haggai 2:15 asked the people to "consider from this day onward."

The people were to consider cause and effect. God said they had spent so much time worried about building their houses, about planting their fields, and about harvesting their food that they had forgotten who gave them abundance. In several places in this short book, God said He sent a drought on the land to thwart the labor of the people. This was not malicious, but it was meant as a way to remind the people from where their blessing truly came. God promised that He would give them grain, new wine, oil, and anything they needed if they had their priorities right and focused on God.

This reminds us poignantly of Jesus' words in the Sermon on the Mount. Matthew 6:25 says, "Do not be worried about your life, *as to* what you will you will eat or what you will drink; nor for your body, *as to* what you will put on. Is not life more than food, and the body more than clothing?"

In Matthew 6:33 Jesus summed up this thought by saying, "But seek first His kingdom and His righteousness, and all these things will be added to you." Haggai is a short book teaching us the same principles that we see Jesus speaking to in Matthew.

Reflection questions:

1. In what ways did the Jews not have their priorities right when they returned from the exile?

2. How was Zerubbabel portrayed in Haggai? Was he a positive character? Why or why not?

3. Is anything wrong with people building their own houses and planting food for themselves? Why was this understood to be negative in Haggai?

21

ZECHARIAH

OF THE MINOR PROPHETS, Zechariah may be the most difficult to interpret. It is one of the longest of the Minor Prophets, with fourteen chapters. It pulls on many of the same themes as the other Minor Prophets, but it certainly stands as a pinnacle book among the Minor Prophets and even within the entire Old Testament.

Rather than being in narrative form like Haggai and Jonah, Zechariah maintains a prophetic form with oracles against nations, prophecies of judgment, prophecies of future restoration, and oracles against wickedness.

Similar to Haggai, Zechariah gives specific dates. Verse 1 says, "In the eighth month of the second year of Darius, the word of the LORD came to Zechariah the prophet."

Both Zechariah's father's and grandfather's names were also given. Time stamps are given not only in verse 1 but elsewhere, such as Zechariah 1:7, which speaks about the twenty-fourth day of the eleventh month of the same year. In fact, it is interesting to note that the word of the Lord came to both Haggai and Zechariah in the second year of Darius, with two very different messages. The timeline of Zechariah goes past Haggai. Zechariah 7:1 mentions the fourth year of Darius.

STRUCTURE

The structure of the book is debated. It does not divide easily into sections. The first portion of the book, the first six verses, is a call to repentance. From Zechariah 1:7 through the end of chapter 6 eight visions are given.

The difficulty with this book is the interpretation for these eight visions. Some of these visions are easier to understand than others. In chapter 3, a vision was given of Joshua the high priest, who was also mentioned as being the high priest in Haggai. Zechariah was given a vision of Joshua standing before the Angel of the Lord, but Satan was also standing at his right hand accusing him.

Similar to Isaiah 6, where Isaiah's iniquity was taken away after an angel touched his lips with a hot coal, the text of Zechariah says the iniquity of Joshua was taken away so that he might perform his duty as the high priest.

However, some of the other visions are more difficult to understand. Zechariah 5 describes a vision of a flying scroll that was twenty cubits long and ten cubits wide, a cubit being about eighteen inches. This flying scroll was a curse against anyone who swore falsely and anyone who was a thief, consuming the house of any such person.

After these eight visions, chapter 7 calls for justice and mercy. It is important to note that chapter 7 begins with a new time stamp, the fourth year of King Darius. This helps us to see the structural break between Zechariah 1–6 and 7. Chapter 8 speaks about the future restoration of Zion and should be linked in structure with chapter 7, both speaking about fasting being turned into celebration.

Chapters 9 and 10 speak of the future restoration of Israel and judgment on Israel's enemies. Chapters 11 through 14 contrast the false leaders of Israel, who destroyed the people, and the true King of Israel, who was pierced for His people. Although the structure has been debated, the following breakdown will prove helpful:

Zechariah 1:1–6	The call to repentance
Zechariah 1:7–6:15	The eight visions
Zechariah 7:1–8:23	Fasting turned into celebration
Zechariah 9:1–14:21	False shepherds vs. the True Shepherd

PURPOSE

Zechariah gave a stark contrast between the false leaders of Israel, depicted as shepherds who did not care for their flock, and the true coming Shepherd of Israel, who will take care of His people. Zechariah spoke a good deal to the destruction and devastation that would come upon Israel because of the wickedness of their rulers.

Within this metaphor of the shepherd and the sheep, we find the well-known verse, Zechariah 13:7, "Strike the Shepherd that the sheep may be scattered." Several prophecies were given of future leaders in Israel who would devastate the people. A prophecy was given that two-thirds of Israel would be cut off, and one-third of Israel would remain. Those remaining would call upon the name of God and be the people of God (Zech. 13:9).

Even though Zechariah can be difficult to fully comprehend, at times it makes specific and clear claims about the day of the Lord. For this reason, Zechariah is one of the most essential and important books, along with Daniel and Revelation, to understand the day of the Lord.

> **Zechariah Purpose Statement:** Even though the false shepherds and rulers devastate Israel, Israel will be purified, and their true Shepherd will come to them.

Theme

The key theme in Zechariah is the coming Shepherd who will deliver the people. This deliverance would come amid great turmoil and distress. Zechariah made great claims about the turmoil that would come upon Israel. This all was in conjunction with the day of the Lord. God was seen as the great Deliverer who would save His people in the last hour. After many false shepherds and ungodly leaders would devastate Israel, the true Shepherd would come on the scene, bringing full and final deliverance for Israel.

This deliverance was described in terms of the redemption of Israel. It was not just that God would save Israel from its enemies. God would redeem the people so that they would be faithful to Him.

Before this deliverance would take place, Zechariah described Israel as being scattered over all the world. In this deliverance, God would bring all of Israel back to their own land to such an extent that there will not even be room for all of them in the land (Zech. 10:10).

Before this deliverance, the people would be in anguish. The deliverance would bring their full and final joy (10:7). Before their deliverance, Israel's enemies devastated them without repercussion (11:5). After their deliverance, God would not only devastate Israel's enemies, but God would also punish all the wicked leaders who sought their own gain to the detriment of their people.

This deliverance is depicted in Zechariah in conjunction with the true Shepherd who was to come. No deliverance would be complete without the true Ruler who would forever guide and rule the people in justice and equity.

Zechariah 12:10 is a beautiful passage that says Israel would look on the One they had pierced and would mourn for Him. They would weep bitterly because He had been pierced. All Israel would turn to follow this true Shepherd. Zechariah 13:1 says, "In that day a fountain will be opened for the house of David and for the inhabitants of Jerusalem, for sin and for impurity."

This is a similar picture to the one that Revelation 22 paints of the river of the water of life that comes out from the throne of God and is for the healing of the nations. Revelation 22:3 says, "There will no longer be any curse; and the throne of God and of the Lamb will be in it, and His bond-servants will serve Him."

Zechariah 13, similarly, spoke of the true Shepherd who would rule His people, the fountain of water, and the fact that all idolatry would be cut off and remembered no more. Zechariah 13:2 says, "I will cut off the names of the idols from the land, and they will no longer be remembered; and I will also remove the prophets and the unclean spirit from the land." There would no longer be any false prophets who will deceive the people.

Zechariah 14 paints a vivid picture of this day of the Lord and of the true Shepherd ruling from Jerusalem. Verse 9 says the Lord will be king over all the earth. Jerusalem will be exalted, and a plague will go out against those who fight against Israel and against the true Shepherd.

The prophecies in Zechariah can be difficult to understand. But some of the prophecies in Zechariah are clear and straightforward. This is especially true in the latter portions of the book. From these prophecies, we get a vivid description of a time yet to come when the true Shepherd of Israel will rule the entire earth from Jerusalem with perfect equity, righteousness, and justice.

Reflection questions:

1. Why do you think some prophecies in Zechariah are so difficult to interpret, and other prophecies are clear and straightforward?

2. How is the true Shepherd of Israel described in Zechariah, and how does that point to both the first and second comings of Christ?

3. How does Zechariah describe the day of the Lord? What are the details of the day of the Lord that Zechariah brings into clear focus?

22

Malachi

When studying the short book of Malachi, the joke is often told that Malachi is the Italian prophet. If you pronounce the "ch" as you would expect it to be pronounced in English, the name does sound Italian. However, the interesting thing about Malachi is that the name in Hebrew simply means "my messenger."

While Malachi could have been the proper name of this prophet, we can also understand Malachi could have been simply a title. The prophet just described himself as the messenger of God. Therefore, in Hebrew, Malachi 1:1 can be read as, "The oracle of the word of the Lord to Israel through Malachi." It can also be read as, "The oracle of the word of the Lord to Israel by My messenger."

This play on the name is also seen in a well-known text in chapter 3. Malachi 3:1 says, "Behold, I am going to send My messenger, and he will clear the way before Me."

While Malachi was a messenger of God, and even his name simply means "my messenger," he pointed to a messenger who would prepare the way for the Messiah.

Structure

The structure of the book can be seen in several different discourses, which are bookended by a short introduction and the conclusion, which speaks about a coming Elijah, the prophet. In Malachi 1:2, God said that He loved Israel. The people immediately responded and ask how God has loved them. God pointed to the decision He made to choose Israel and stated, "I have loved Jacob; but I have hated Esau" (Mal. 1:2–3). This passage was picked up by Paul in Romans when Paul spoke about the sovereign choice of God in election.

The second discourse started after 1:6, when God called the people to account for their wicked sacrifices. God said the people had not honored Him as their Father, but had given lame and sick animals as a minimal offering to the Lord. God said He would not accept the offerings of the people.

The third discourse began in Malachi 2:10 where God accused the people of being unfaithful like an adulteress. Malachi 2:17 began the next discourse in which God warned the people of coming judgment.

Malachi 3:6 is the next section that accuses the people of robbing God. God said that if the people would just give generously from their hearts that He would bless them beyond measure. But because they withheld and tried to rob God, they had nothing.

The final discourse begins in Malachi 3:13, which gives hope to the righteous. This section to the last verse of the book told the righteous that they would be remembered and vindicated. All evildoers would be destroyed. All hypocrisy would come to light. The day of the Lord would bring ultimate justice for those who truly followed after God.

Purpose

The purpose of Malachi was to call the people to repentance. Malachi sought to bring the wickedness of the people to light to show them their need for repentance. Whenever their wickedness was brought to light, they tried to twist the facts and their actions to make themselves look better.

This hypocrisy and twisting of the truth would be brought into judgment. Like in many of the Minor Prophets, the day of the Lord was emphasized as that time in which God would bring full and final judgment.

A key purpose that we need to see in Malachi is also the emphasis upon the coming prophet. This is seen in Malachi 3:1 as well as Malachi 4:5. This coming messenger would mark a milestone in the timeline of the coming day of the Lord, a day when time has run out for the wicked.

Malachi Purpose Statement: Israel was warned of coming final judgment against hypocrisy and unfaithfulness to their covenant with God.

Themes

A key theme of Malachi is the hypocrisy of the people. God indicted the people for various sins, but the people claimed innocence. In Malachi 1:6, God said He was a Father to Israel, but Israel did not honor Him as their Father. Israel responded with, "How have we despised your name?"

No matter what indictment was given against the people, they immediately responded by asking how they had done wrong. They took no responsibility for their wickedness. This culminated with the statement, "You have wearied the Lord with your words" (Mal. 2:17). God had grown tired of the people not repenting or taking responsibility for their wickedness. They tried to twist their actions to make them appear good. However, the entire time, they demonstrated their hypocrisy. Their greed, selfishness, and corruption compelled them to act in wickedness, violating God's commands. When God called them to account, they did not confess or repent.

Description is given of Israel acting as though they were repenting. Malachi 2:13 says they covered the Lord's altar with tears. They begged God for blessing, but God did not give in. They asked why not. God responded by saying that they had been unfaithful to Him.

Another theme found in Malachi, which is similar to Zechariah, is that of the wickedness of the leaders of Israel, specifically the priests. God said they act corruptly and had caused many to stumble by their instruction (Mal. 2:8). Through their evil teaching, that which was evil was thought of as good, and that which was good was thought of as evil (2:17; 3:15).

As in so many of the other Minor Prophets, the day of the Lord was highlighted. Malachi described the day of the Lord as the day that would bring separation between the wicked and the righteous. It would be clear who was wicked and who was righteous. All hypocrisy would be brought to light.

A key text is Malachi 4:5, "Behold, I am going to send you Elijah the prophet before the coming of the great and terrible day of the LORD." In Matthew 11:14 Jesus said that John the Baptist was the Elijah who was to come.

Malachi did not say how long before the day of the Lord that this Elijah would come. He only said that God would send this Elijah before the great and awesome day of the Lord. Malachi, like the other Minor Prophets, described the day of the Lord as a day of devastation and punishment for the wicked, as well as a day of blessing and healing for those who truly followed after God.

Reflection questions:

1. In what way is Malachi a fitting end to the Old Testament, pointing to the coming Messiah?

2. In Matthew 11:14, Jesus said, "If you are willing to accept *it*, John himself is Elijah who was to come." Why do you think Jesus said, "If you are willing to accept it"? How does this point to the hypocrisy of the people, which is also seen in the message of Malachi?

3. In what ways throughout Malachi did the people try to twist the truth to make themselves look better?

CLC PUBLICATIONS
Fort Washington, PA 19034

This book is published by CLC Publications, an outreach of CLC Ministries International. The purpose of CLC is to make evangelical Christian literature available to all nations so that people may come to faith and maturity in the Lord Jesus Christ. We hope this book has been life changing and has enriched your walk with God through the work of the Holy Spirit. If you would like to know more about CLC, we invite you to visit our website:

www.clcusa.org

To learn more about the remarkable story of the founding of CLC International, we encourage you to read

LEAP OF FAITH

Norman Grubb
Paperback
Size 5 1/4 x 8, Pages 248
ISBN: 978-0-87508-650-7
ISBN (*e-book*): 978-1-61958-055-8

Also in the Christian Life Series from

CLC Publications

BY

Nathan LeMaster

Old Testament Survey I

Genesis to Esther

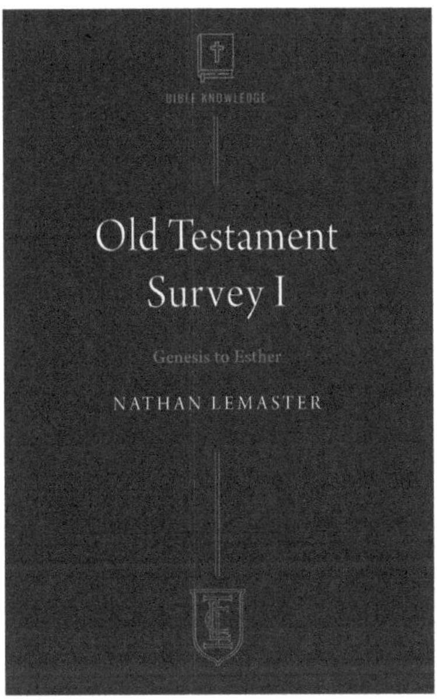

For many believers, the Old Testament is often left in mothballs—a tragedy that shouldn't be allowed to continue. Nathan LeMaster shows the relevance, intricacy, and intention of the Old Testament, seeking to reignite a passion for its study. (Part I—Genesis to Esther.) Part of the Christian Life Series.

Paperback
Size 6 x 9, Pages 128
ISBN: 978-1-61958-365-8
ISBN (*e-book*): 978-1-61958-377-1

New Testament Survey I

Pauline and General Epistles

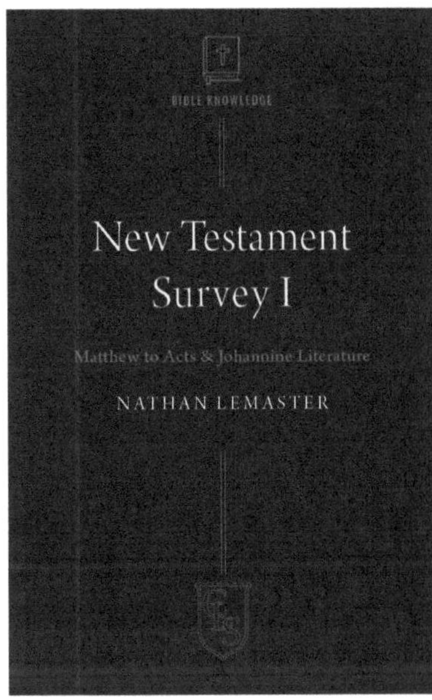

In this first volume of his New Testament Survey (Matthew to Acts, Johannine Literature), Nathan LeMaster helps the reader navigate the Gospels, Acts, and John's letters, demonstrating the relevance, intricacy, and intentionality of the New Testament, while revealing Jesus as its central focus and reigniting a passion for its study.

Paperback
Size 6 x 9, Pages 128
ISBN: 978-1-61958-394-8
ISBN (*e-book*): 978-1-61958-396-2

Coming soon from

CLC Publications

by

Nathan LeMaster

New Testament Survey II
Pauline and General Epistles